INTERNATIONAL ENCYCLOPEDIA OF ART

European Art to 1850

first edition

Tony Lucchesi and Fulvio Palombo

Facts On File, Inc.

INTERNATIONAL ENCYCLOPEDIA OF ART
EUROPEAN ART TO 1850

Text copyright © 1997 Tony Lucchesi and Fulvio Palombo
Copyright © 1997 Cynthia Parzych Publishing, Inc.
Design, maps, timeline design copyright © 1997 Cynthia Parzych Publishing, Inc.

Cataloging-in-Publication Data available on request from
Facts On File, Inc.

Facts on File books are available at special discounts when purchased in bulk quantities
for businesses, associations, institutions or sales promotions. Please call our Special
Sales Department in New York at 212/967-8800 or 800/322-8755.

This is a Mirabel Book produced by:
Cynthia Parzych Publishing, Inc.
648 Broadway
New York, NY 10012

Edited by: Frances Helby
Designed by: Dorchester Typesetting Group Ltd.
Printed and bound in Spain by: Imschoot Graphic Service

Front cover: Giotto painted *Deposition of Christ*, part of a series of frescoes for the
Arena Chapel in Padua, Italy, about 1304-13.

10 9 8 7 6 5 4 3 2 1

Contents

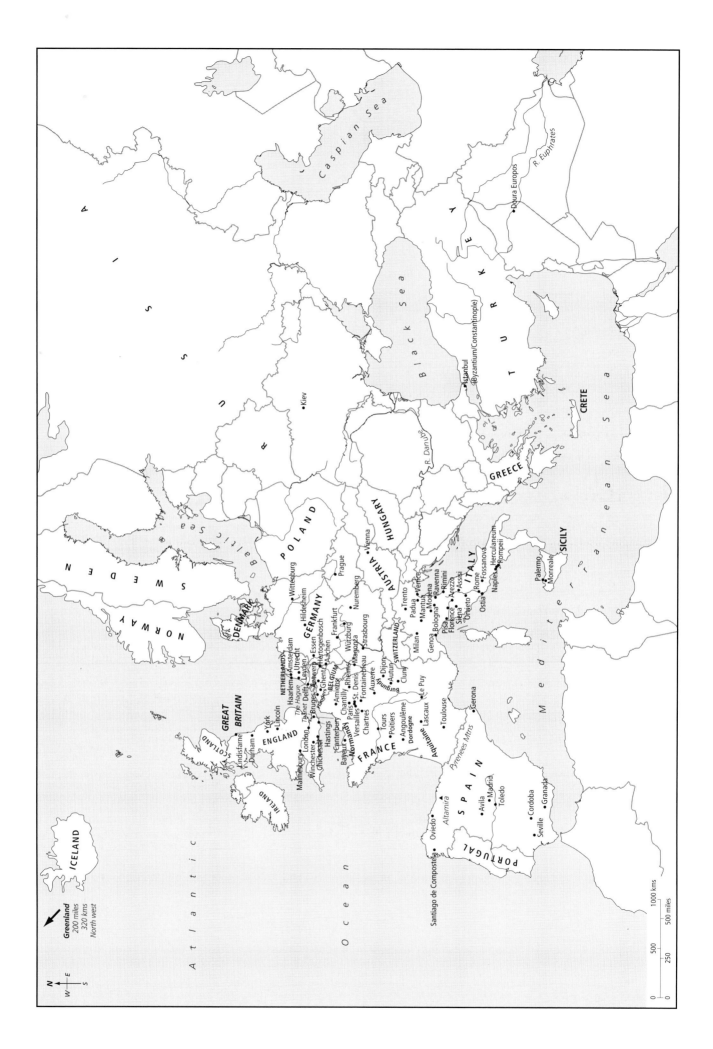

Introduction

Is there a beginning of art or an exact place in time we can pinpoint when making art began? Probably not. Since the Bronze Age, between four thousand and two thousand years B.C., people have been producing their own forms of art.

To be able to understand the many kinds of art discussed in this volume, it is necessary to understand the intentions of the artists in the context of the societies in which they lived and what was happening in the world around them.

Art expressions mean different things to different viewers. The animal forms of a Celtic gilt-bronze buckle had a symbolic meaning for the original Celt who wore it. A modern visitor to the museum where the buckle is now displayed may merely find it attractive. The Byzantine mosaics of the sixth century A.D., representing Christian figures, were stark, flat, stylized forms executed in gold and vibrant colors. They were the expression of the intense, austere and authoritarian spirituality of the time. They would not have expressed the Christian spirit which produced Gothic cathedrals almost 500 years later.

In Europe, the combination of two major historical events, the birth of Christianity in the Mediterranean in the first century A.D. and the decline of the Roman Empire in the fifth century, brought about an explosion of visual art. Early Christians could not help but invent a new and vigorous style of expression, given the intense fervor, energy and sense of purpose which came from their conversion. Marauding barbarian

Timeline

This timeline lists some of the important events, both historical (listed above the time bar) and art historical (below) that have been mentioned in this book. While every event cannot be mentioned it is hoped that this diagram will help the reader to understand at a glance how these events relate in time.

64: Christians are persecuted by the Emperor Nero.

79: Mount Vesuvius erupts and buries Pompeii and Herculaneum.

313: Christianity is legalized in the Roman Empire.

330: The capital of the Roman Empire moves to Byzantium.

432: The Celtic Church is founded in Ireland.

711: Spain is conquered by the Muslims.

726–843: The Iconoclastic controversy begins.

800: Charlemagne is crowned Holy Roman Emperor and feudalism begins to be established.

911: The Viking lord, Rollo, is granted land that becomes known as Normandy.

from about 1000: Europe is gradually repopulated and revitalized.

from 35,000 B.C.: Paleolithic hunter-gatherer people live in groups in caves.

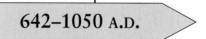

35,000–8000 B.C. **64–576 A.D.** **642–1050 A.D.**

from 35,000 B.C.: Bone objects are carved and decorated.

from 8000 B.C.: Cave paintings are made in France, Spain and Sicily.

until 79: Frescoes are painted at Pompeii and Herculaneum.

32–313: Early Christian art develops.

527–76: Byzantine mosaic art reaches its greatest height during the Justinian Golden Age.

late 600s to 793: Lindisfarne Abbey produces illuminated manuscripts and book covers.

from 711: Arab culture and architecture spreads through Spain.

726–843: The Iconoclastic Controversy leads to the destruction of most religious images in the Roman Empire.

late 900s and early 1000s: A great artistic revival under Otto I results in the Romanesque style. Byzantine influence spreads to Eastern Europe and the first Christian art appears in Russia.

tribes settled in all parts of central and northern Europe as the Roman Empire declined. These tribes possessed an artistic language, but lacked the ability to take their art forms beyond ornamentation.

The power of the drawn, painted and sculpted image over the mind of man cannot be overestimated. For example, around the middle of the eighth century A.D., the iconoclastic controversy caused the destruction of most Byzantine figure art. For more than a hundred years, the depiction of images in the likeness of man was forbidden.

Europe in the early Middle Ages was devastated by the divided and weakened Christian empire of Rome and years of barbarian invasions. Europe was saved from total destruction when the charismatic, Frankish King Charlemagne was crowned ruler of Europe, in 800. During Charlemagne's reign, western Europe was unified for the first time. Charlemagne's heirs, however, failed to maintain this unity. Europe descended to a low level and the Church lost most of its authority.

The origins of the Romanesque style may be traced to the year 500. The western Roman Empire was threatened by invading barbarians. In the monasteries literature, scientific investigations, the practice of alchemy and the study of astronomy continued. Illuminated manuscripts were produced illustrated with beautiful human figures, animals and interlace patterns. The monastic center of Cluny in France, where the Romanesque style made its debut, was influential in restoring the Catholic Church's prestige about the year 1000.

During the Middle Ages, the Romanesque tradition spread mostly to Italy and France and absorbed Celtic forms. The Byzantine style was suppressed by the Persians and Arabs in the eastern Roman Empire, but experienced a revival through the Eastern Orthodox Church, particularly in Russia. The Christianized northern Celtic forms of art were influenced by the

---

1000s to 1100s: The Italian navies free trade routes, trade guilds begin to be established and the middle class begins to appear.

1060–91: The Normans complete their occupation of Sicily.

1066: William of Normandy conquers England.

1096–1192: The three major crusades take place.

1098: The Cistercian order of monks is founded.

1050–1200 A.D.

1050 onwards: The Romanesque style predominates throughout Europe with strong regional variations.

1053: An era of church building begins with the foundation of the cathedral at Pisa.

1077: The Bayeux Tapestry is completed.

1200s: Imperial power declines and the power of city-states in Italy and the merchant class rises.

1271: Marco Polo sets out for China to explore trade routes. Trade by land and sea intensifies.

1347–50: The Great Plague, or the Black Death, ravages Europe.

1201–1399 A.D.

1137: The Gothic style is established with the rebuilding of the Abbey church of St. Denis near Paris.

by 1250: The Gothic style spreads throughout most of Europe.

1308–11: Figures enclosed in an architectural interior are painted for the first time in Duccio's *Annunciation of the Death of the Virgin*.

1300s: A distinct French Gothic style develops.

1444: The printing press is invented.

1517: Martin Luther sets the Protestant Reformation in motion.

mid-1500s: The Counter-Reformation of the Roman Catholic Church begins in southern Europe.

1568: The Netherlands rebels against Spain.

1400–1579 A.D.

early 1400s: A Europe-wide International Gothic style suddenly appears and secular art begins. The Flemish school of painting flourishes.

1402–52: Ghiberti's two sets of doors for the baptistery at Florence exemplify the change from the Gothic to the Renaissance style.

1508–12: The ceiling of the Sistine Chapel is painted.

from 1517: Religious imagery and churches in northern Europe are destroyed.

late 1500s: Italian artists react against Renaissance ideals and the Mannerist style appears.

Byzantine style. They became the tradition throughout most of northern Europe. There these art forms advanced, particularly in Ireland.

The countries of the lower basin of the Mediterranean, as well as Spain and part of southern Italy, were for a time under Islamic control. After about 700 A.D., Islamic art was confined mainly to these countries.

By the end of the tenth century, Europe was in a great state of political, social and cultural transition. For the next 250 years in western Europe, the feudal system became a way of life. This was a period of civic unity and a religious-inspired artistic revolution blended northern, southern and eastern cultures. In this period of the Middle Ages, artistic energy found its expression in the Romanesque and Gothic styles. At the beginning of the fourteenth century, the Italian artist Giotto brought a new vision to painting.

In the fourteenth century people began to focus on the earth and universe. With this new way of looking at the world the Renaissance style in art came about. Renaissance art began to appear at the start of the fifteenth century in Florence, Italy. The city blossomed with a vital, humane spirit. The Renaissance was responsible for some of the greatest works of genius in painting and sculpture the world has ever known.

After the Counter-Reformation, a period of rigid reform in the sixteenth century, the Catholic Church gave artists greater freedom of expression. In the seventeenth century Rome became the center of the Baroque art movement in Europe. In the eighteenth century, the Baroque style gave way to a lighter, Rococo style in France and England.

In the eighteenth century in France and England, the Enlightenment, generated the atmosphere which gave rise to Neo-Classical art and Romanticism, styles which lasted until the nineteenth century.

---

by 1580: The Counter-Reformation is secure in Italy and Spain.

by early 1600s: Modern science is established.

1618–48: The Thirty Years' War involves much of Europe. The population of Germany is cut in half.

by late 1600s: France replaces Spain as the most powerful nation in Europe.

1580–1682 A.D.

from 1580: Baroque art of the Counter-Reformation appears in Italy.

1618–48: The Thirty Years' War causes destruction of art and buildings.

by mid-1600s: Baroque art reaches most of Europe.

late 1600s: Baroque Classicism flourishes in France.

from 1680s: Artistic activity revives and reconstruction begins in the areas ravaged by the Thirty Years' War.

1683: The Turks begin to be pushed out of Europe.

1700s: The intellectual movement of the Enlightenment flourishes throughout the century in France and Great Britain.

1683–1749 A.D.

by 1700: There is a great divide between artists who believe in the supremacy of color and those who believe in the supremacy of line.

1700s: The Rococo style develops.

1776: The American Declaration of Independence is signed.

1789: The French Revolution begins.

by 1793: Russian expansion leads to its domination of central Europe as far as the Black Sea.

1800–10: The Industrial Revolution begins.

1750–1850 A.D.

1750–1850: The Neo-Classic and Romantic styles flourish.

1790–1830: Romanticism reaches its height.

1 Paleolithic Cave Art

▲ *This great frieze of aurochs, horses and deer painted in black and red, made between 30,000 and 25,000 B.C., was found in a cave at Lascaux, France. Cavemen made the animals the right size to fit the space. Sometimes they were drawn in outline and other times as a solid mass of fuzzy, painted color.*

Social Life

Towards the end of the Ice Age, in about 35,000 B.C., people in Europe began to live in caves. Archeologists have found hearths and tombs dating from this time. Caves provided enclosed, protective spaces and more stable living conditions. This encouraged a more personal and warmer group life for cave dwellers. It also would have required the knowledge of how to contain and control fire. The fire would have made life easier providing warmth, a means of cooking and a social focus for a group. ■

The oldest forms of art that have been found were made about 35,000 B.C. They are colored, decorated, bone and ivory objects and were found in caves in northern Spain and southwest France. Extraordinary examples of the paintings and relief carvings made in about 20,000 B.C. have been found on the walls and ceilings of caves, such as those in Altamira, northern Spain, and in Lascaux, in the Dordogne region of southwest France. Many of the pictures show hunting scenes, with stick figures for men, and animals drawn with almost perfect proportions and rounded form. Paleolithic artists were capable of extracting the essential spirit of the animals and capturing it in their art with extraordinary power.

It is more than likely that cave artists reproduced animal images by copying the same models over and over again. It seems to have been important to paint the type of animal in its general appearance rather than individual animals. For example, a single reindeer would represent all reindeer and not a particular one seen on a certain day.

Paleolithic people probably felt small and insignificant in the great, unknown and unexplored world. Making painted images might have made them feel that in some way they could possess what they saw. Perhaps the painted images helped to make a closer tie between them, the world and nature. Perhaps they thought they could make their presence felt more strongly in the universe through the signs or marks of their paintings.

▲ *This bison, found in a cave at Altamira, Spain, was painted about 15,000 to 12,000 B.C. with remarkable accuracy. It is full of energy and life.*

Mural Art

Prehistoric cave art was developed by the hunters of large animals in western Europe, especially the French Pyrenees, the western Cantabrian Pyrenees area in Spain and in Sicily. As well as paintings, low relief sculptures and incised drawings or engravings can be found in this mural art. In addition to animals, there are human figures dressed up in animal skins or with grotesque head coverings. These figures might have inspired dancing and initiation ceremonies, represented sorcerers or gods or were simply disguised as animals to fool their prey. In eastern Spain the rock paintings show men engaged in war, hunting and dancing. ■

Tools

Paleolithic man made spear heads of flint, bone, ivory and antler. Flint blades and burins (chisel-headed tools), were needed to incise rock for their art work. Handaxes and wooden spears with pointed stone heads had been developed as early as 400,000 to 300,000 B.C. The skill of making tools grew slowly. ■

◀ *The* Venus of Laussel, *made between 30,000 and 25,000 B.C. in Laussel, southwest France, shows the artist had a remarkable knowledge of the female form. She was probably a fertility figure and holds a horn in her right hand. A bison horn filled with blood is still a fertility symbol in some parts of Africa today. The impressive figure, produced in high relief, was coaxed out of the rock surface by its prehistoric creator.*

Early men and women might have tried to understand their unexplored, almost incomprehensible world by acknowledging an unseen, supernatural and sacred world of the spirit. By painting animals, people may well have thought they could possess the unseen animal spirits. They may have believed that animals had the secret both to this world and to the supernatural world. Figures painted in black and wearing animal skins and head coverings, are either hunters using camouflage or may be evidence that suggests magic and ritual played an important part in the lives of Paleolithic people. These people also made small engraved objects from bones, and statuettes with abstract decorations. The decorations perhaps are also related to their ideas of the supernatural world.

Pictures made in caves, in deeply hidden recesses, were safe from the weather and from intruders. Hunters may have painted their hunting scenes before they went out to hunt. Perhaps they showed animals being killed in their paintings to symbolically take away the power of the living animals. Images of dead animals were represented by overlapping them with drawings or paintings of other animals. They used charcoal to work on the animal forms until they reached a satisfactory image. Color was added using natural materials, usually ground minerals. In some of the paintings, the men are disguised by wearing masks of one animal and skins of another. Through their paintings, the hunters perhaps also gathered courage and strength to confront the terrifying beasts they needed to kill for their food, armed only with their primitive weapons.

Cave paintings may also have been a sort of fertility magic. People may have thought that all life sprang from the earth and the deep caves were its womb. They may have put images of the animals they hunted in the womb of the earth, so they would be born again in real life in great numbers.

2 Early Christian Art

Suppression and Persecution

Life for Christians under Roman rule was uncertain and threatened by continual persecution. In general, the Roman Empire was tolerant of all religions. Nevertheless, history reveals there were uprisings in the empire by repressed groups for hundreds of years which often were put down by persecution, torture or death. During the reign of the emperor Nero (37–68 A.D.), Christians suffered the worst period of persecution. The torture and martyrdom of the followers of Jesus Christ, the apostles Peter and Paul, in about 66 A.D., marks this period. Martyrs, people killed by the authorities for their beliefs, became the heroes of Christianity and subjects of Christian art. ■

▲ *Roman fresco paintings were the source of the early Christian catacomb art. In the painted frescoes of the Villa of the Mysteries at Pompeii, of about 50 B.C., monumental figures stand out against a deep red, abstract background. The precise drawing, a clear definition of the volumes and the use of dark and light all demonstrate the highest achievement of Pompeian painting.*

Under the emperor Trajan, who ruled from 98 to 117 A.D., the Roman Empire reached its greatest size and power. Its territories extended from Egypt and the Middle East to all the lands around the Mediterranean, across western Europe, to France and the British Isles.

A new religion, Christianity, took hold in Syria, Phoenicia and Palestine in the the first century A.D. Christianity is based on the teachings of Jesus Christ (4 B.C.–32 or 33 A.D.), set down in the Bible. Christians believe Jesus is the Son of God and is himself divine. They believe that if they follow Jesus' teachings they will have eternal life after death.

The Romans had their own religion and for nearly 300 years they forbade the representation of Christian imagery in their empire. Christian images were produced in secrecy, and, in spite of intolerance and persecution, the spread of Christianity gathered momentum, throughout the entire Mediterranean, from Armenia to Spain. Its expansion changed the course of history.

Christian art was first made in small communities skirting Alexandria in Egypt, where it is known as Coptic art. It flourished there from 190 to 642 A.D. Coptic art reflected the Egyptian and Ethiopian interpretation of Christianity.

Little Christian art has survived from before 200 A.D., but examples from the third century A.D. can be found in a Christian house in the town of Doura Europos, on the upper Euphrates River, and in the catacombs in Rome. The catacombs were underground tunnels used as tombs and secret places to meet and worship. Jewish converts to Christianity brought the idea of the catacombs with them when they came to Italy from the Middle East.

Fresco paintings have been found in both Doura Europos and

The Catacombs

In the Middle East, especially in Palestine, catacombs had been used as tombs for burying a single family for centuries before Christianity. The Roman catacombs, however, were used for burying an entire Christian community. They were also used as secret places for Christian worship, and as hiding places in times of persecution. Long passageways meandered for miles underground, branching out into small rooms probably used for ceremonial services, such as baptism. ■

▲ *In a detail from the St. Priscilla catacombs in Rome (about 200 A.D.), Christ is dressed in a Roman tunic, like the figures in Roman frescoes.*

Early Churches

The new position of Christianity after 380 A.D. as the state religion of the Roman Empire led to the building of churches with spacious interiors for Christian worship. The Roman basilica, a great, covered space used as a market or tribunal, provided a suitable model for the builders of these early Christian churches. The plain brick surfaces of the exteriors contrasted with the beauty and brightness of the colorful mosaics and precious marble decorations inside. ■

In this ▶ mosaic from the church of St. Costanza, Rome, about 350 A.D., plants and birds were created with special attention to accuracy.

Rome. The Doura Europos frescoes are made in the Coptic style. The paintings in the catacombs at Rome show the influence of Roman fresco painting. The best examples of Roman paintings are found in houses at the towns of Pompeii and Herculaneum, near Naples, that were buried by a volcanic eruption in 79 A.D. and only uncovered in the eighteenth century. Pompeii's frescoes use brilliant reds and yellows, and their themes were taken from Greek and Roman mythology.

We do not know who the early Christian artists were. The catacomb artists were not highly trained but they did try to capture the realism and some of the illusion of depth of the Pompeii-style paintings. They were not interested in revealing the exact form of their subjects but seemed more concerned with what the figures represented. These frescoes give some idea of the early Christians' spirit and attitude to their faith. Early Christians disdained the material world; they were preoccupied with the inner spiritual world and with eternal salvation.

▲ *A Christian sculptor carved these scenes from Christ's Passion in the Roman style on a sarcophagus around 350 A.D. The sculptor depicts Christ, just as the Romans might have represented one of their gods.*

Roman pagan art was the style that predominated throughout the Roman Empire. Christian artists used pagan symbols to hide the identity of their images, or else used symbols which would mean nothing to non-Christians. The peacock, which represented the bird of the goddess Juno for the Romans, became the symbol of everlasting life for the Christians; faith was symbolized by a fish and the Church was shown as a ship. In this way artists were able to express the abstract concept of faith for the first time in the western world.

Because of suppression by the Romans, Christian art was not seen by many people in the first two centuries of Christianity. The repression and persecution lasted until the early years of the fourth century A.D. The emperor Constantine (274–337 A.D.) understood the strength of Christianity. In 313 A.D., he declared that the Christian religion was to be permitted. In 380 A.D., it was made the state religion of the Roman Empire.

3 Byzantine Art

Daily Life

Small farmers and free villagers outside the major urban centers in the Byzantine world faced heavy taxes and were often threatened by hostile invaders. Large estates were owned by powerful land-owners. People in debt to a landowner might barter away their freedom to pay their debts. Slavery was found at every level of society in spite of the fact that it was prohibited. In the countryside, villagers lived on the bare essentials that they produced. The wealthy minor-ity enjoyed a life surrounded by works of art. ■

◀ *Hagia Sophia dedicated in 537, in Constantinople, is the finest example of Byzantine domed churches. Only the best materials from all parts of the empire were used to build it. The exterior is simple, but the interior is astonishing because of its lightness and grandiosity. A brilliant light is produced by the windows in the dome.*

In the fourth century A.D., the western half of the Roman Empire was battered by continual invasions of barbarians from northern and eastern Europe. Rome was not spared. In 330, the Roman emperor Constantine the Great, moved the center of the Christian world from Rome to the Greek city of Byzantium and saved the empire from complete destruction. Those parts of the Roman Empire ruled from Byzantium became known as the Byzantine Empire. Byzantium was renamed Constantinople, or Constantine's city, and became the greatest, most fortified city in the world. Today, it is known as Istanbul, Turkey.

By the fifth and sixth centuries, Constantinople had become the thriving and powerful center of the Roman Empire, while the rest of western Europe remained prey to the barbarian invaders. The emperor Justinian, (approx. 482–565) recovered much of the territory the barbarians had conquered so that the empire included Greece and the Balkan countries

The Iconoclastic Controversy

The iconoclastic controversy arose from a decree issued in 726 by Emperor Leo III (approx. 680–741). The decree forbade the portrayal of all religious images and required the destruction of those that already existed. The prohibition lasted until 843. Many Byzantine artists emigrated away from the eastern part of the Byzantine Empire, which was at the center of the conflict. They moved towards the western provinces of the empire which included Ravenna and Rome. Almost all the existing Byzantine art, sculptures, paintings and mosaics were destroyed in the east. No illuminated bibles or manuscripts on the lives of the saints were produced for a hundred years. The iconoclastic controversy was one of the causes of the eleventh century sepa-ration of Orthodox Christianity in the eastern part of the empire from Catholicism in the western part. ■

▲ *The church of St. Apollinare in Classe was consecrated in 549. The simple basilica church is typical of early Byzantine building. The windows are made of alabaster which allows a soft and delicate light to pour on the apse mosaics. The floor mosaics, of which little remains today, consisted of geometric patterns. Inside the church are important sarcophagi from the fifth to the eighth century. They show the development of sculpture during these centuries.*

This ivory ▶ throne, carved in low relief, was a gift from Emperor Justinian to Maximian, the archbishop of Ravenna, in the first half of the sixth century. The carving reveals the work of the hands of several artists.

Ravenna

Today, some of the few surviving examples of Byzantine art and architecture of the sixth century can be seen in the city of Ravenna, on the east coast of Italy. Ravenna survived the devastation and destruction that the rest of the Byzantine Empire suffered because of its isolated position, east of the Apennine Mountains and facing the Adriatic Sea. From 402 to 476 Ravenna became the sumptuous capital of the western part of the empire. The churches of St. Vitale, St. Apollinare Nuovo, St. Apollinare in Classe, the baptisteries and the archbishop's chapel, with their magnificent mosaic decorations, give a clear idea of the splendors of Byzantine art. ■

south of the Danube River, much of the Middle East and Egypt, Italy, the Mediterranean islands, North Africa and southern Spain. Artistic activity flourished with a growing need for art and architecture.

The greatest Byzantine art was made for churches and its most significant expression was in mosaics. Mosaic artists tried to capture the calm and mystery of the heavenly world in their work. Christ, the Virgin Mary, saints and apostles were all represented as austere and rigid figures decorated in brilliantly colored geometric designs.

Byzantine sculptors confined their work to relief sculpture. In the middle of the seventh century the figure disappeared completely from sculpture and was replaced by symbolic, decorative motifs. In the eighth century, the use of the technique of incising reduced reliefs to flat, engraved drawings on smooth marble surfaces.

In eastern Europe the first wave of Byzantine influence was felt in Russia in 987, when the Czar Vladimir I (approx. 956–1015) accepted Christianity. The eleventh century, saw production of the earliest Russian icons, or sacred painted images, illuminated manuscripts and the beginnings of Russian church architecture.

This is a ▶ portion of a mosaic from San Vitale in Ravenna, Empress Theodora and Her Attendants produced about 547.

4 Early Medieval Art

This is the ▶ Bewcastle Cross located in northeast Cumbria in England. It was originally painted in bright colors probably in the seventh or eighth centuries. It probably provided a place for Christians to stop and meditate.

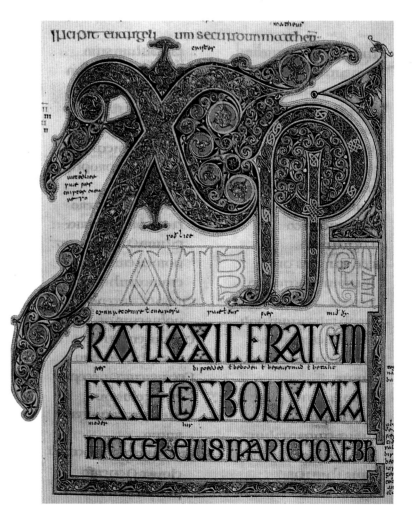

▲ *The Lindisfarne Gospels were written and illuminated by Eadfrith, Bishop of Lindisfarne, between, 698 and 721 A.D. in an original style.*

The Middle Ages in Europe cover about a thousand years of history. The period began at the fall of the western Roman Empire in 476 and ended with the discovery of the Americas in 1492. The early medieval, or Dark Ages, are the 500 years leading up to the year 1000. This was a period of important historical and political events, but was poor in artistic expression. It was a turbulent time of migrations and wars in Europe.

While there was a general artistic decline in Europe in the seventh and eighth centuries, an important artistic contribution was made by barbarian invaders. The art of the barbarians incorporated stylized figures, mostly animals, that were transformed into abstract, decorative motifs. The origins of this art are found in two different cultures:

14

▲ *This Viking ship from Oseberg, Norway, is a splendid example of beautifully carved wood with intricate designs. It was a funerary ship.*

Viking Daily Life

The Vikings were accomplished seafarers and farmers. The designs of their fine ships allowed them to land on many kinds of beachheads and penetrate deep inland up rivers. The Vikings took great care over cultivating their land. Hunting and fishing were daily tasks. On every farm there was a blacksmith. Often these smiths were fine craftspeople. ■

Scythian and Celtic. The Scythians, nomads and warriors, came from central Asia and settled on the Caspian and Black Seas, about 3000 B.C. Celts were of Indo-European origin, and were first found in central Europe around 1000 B.C. The Celts moved through France, Spain, Great Britain and Ireland.

The Celts are best known for their animal art and ribbon patterns called interlacing which were decorative and had symbolic meanings. The Celts engraved and embossed their interlacing designs in bronze, gold and silver and wove interlacing designs into their fabrics.

Ireland was converted to Christianity by St. Patrick who went there about 432 A.D. Relatively insulated from the barbarian invasions of the sixth and seventh century, Celtic Ireland was able to develop an original art form based on the designs of the ancient Celts.

With the departure of the Romans and invasion by the Germanic Saxons from northern Europe, England reverted to paganism. Irish Christians began to come to England, Wales and Scotland as missionaries. The abbey of Lindisfarne, a small island off Northumberland, northeast England, was founded, in 635. Lindisfarne was a center of monastic culture and art and was famous for its scriptorium, or writing school, where monks copied and illuminated sacred Christian books. Illuminating the Gospels, which tell of Jesus' life on earth, helped to make them understandable to illiterate Christians.

On June 8, 793 A.D., the abbey of Lindisfarne was sacked and destroyed by the Vikings, marking a new wave of barbarian invasion. The pagan Vikings came from the Scandinavian peninsula and menaced the coasts of Europe for the next two and half centuries. Over-population and the scarcity of cultivated land in Scandinavia were the fundamental reasons for the Viking invasions and expansion. Danish Vikings invaded France, southeastern England, Ireland, Spain and the Mediterranean. Swedish Vikings went east, through Russia and reached Byzantium. Vikings from Norway, the Norsemen, landed first in Scotland and Ireland. They colonized Iceland and Greenland, explored Labrador and probably New England and settled in Newfoundland.

Between the fifth and seventh centuries Viking art was characterized by decorative, intertwined, geometric patterns and animal themes embossed on cast metals. After the seventh century, the continental style of Vendel, in central Sweden, appeared in northern art. This style combined Celtic interlace with intricate geometric patterns and elongated animal torsos designed in ribbons of interlace. Helmets, belts and buckles, scabbards, swords, shields and jewelry were made by Viking artists all over Scandinavia.

◄ *This lion's head from Oseberg, Norway, made in the ninth century, was used for the prow of a warship.*

5 Carolingian and Ottonian Art

▲ *In the Capilla de Villaviciosa in the mosque at Cordoba, Spain, built between 961 and 965 by the Muslims, the interplay of the arches creates a feeling that the viewer is being held back or pushed away from the wall.*

Feudalism

During the reigns of Charlemagne and later Carolingian kings vassals or land-owning subjects provided fighting men to serve the emperor or king. The king gave them land in return. These vassals had vassals of their own who gave their loyalty and service in exchange for land and protection. This system, which reached down to the lowest of the free in society, is often called feudalism. The name comes from the feud or fief which was the land that provided the bond between lord and vassal. ■

Charlemagne (747–814) was responsible for the unification of most of western Europe after centuries of chaos, caused by internal strife and foreign invasion. He crushed the Lombards' power in Italy in 773. In 778, he fought the Arabs who occupied Spain. Later, he defeated the Avars and the Slavs in eastern Europe and the Danes. He supported the papacy against rebellion in Rome and, in gratitude for this protection, Pope Leo III crowned him Charles the Great, Emperor of the Romans, on Christmas Day in the year 800. He was the first emperor crowned in Rome since the fall of the western Roman Empire, in 476. Because he had the pope's blessing he was called the Holy Roman Emperor.

Charlemagne's was a feudal empire based on a hierarchy headed by the emperor, with land divided among lesser dukes and counts. The population of the empire was relatively small and the main occupa-

The Arabs in Spain and Sicily

The Muslims, followers of Islam, the religion founded by Muhammed (approx. 570–632), created a vast empire which embraced Arabia, Syria, Egypt, Palestine and the coast of North Africa. From there the Muslims invaded Spain in the eighth century and Sicily in ninth century. They left traces of their highly evolved civilization and artistic monuments in the countries they occupied. Many Muslims interpreted Islamic writings as forbidding the representation of the human figure and animals in religious art. So the emphasis in most Islamic art was on abstract decorative forms. ■

tion was farming. People lived in small villages usually organized around cathedrals, monasteries and abbeys, the only centers of culture and learning. Charlemagne encouraged the foundation of schools, libraries and scriptoria and invited some of the greatest scholars of the age to an academy he founded. The children of the nobility were permitted to study at these centers.

Charlemagne launched a cultural rebirth program called the Carolingian Renaissance, in which he attempted to bring back classical Roman values. Different artistic expressions were brought together during the Carolingian period. Roman and Byzantine styles predominated in ivory carvings. Celtic, Germanic and other styles are to be found in illuminated manuscripts, sculpture and gold and silver jewelry.

▲ *The* Lindau Gospels Cover *was made in 870 by a Celtic-Germanic goldsmith. It was worked in gold and studded with precious stones.*

Charlemagne's Palace Chapel built between 792 and 805 in Aachen, Germany, was inspired by architecture he saw on his many trips to Italy. This is an interior view of the chapel. ▼

Manuscripts and Book Covers

The surviving Gospel books and illuminated manuscripts from the Carolingian Renaissance period are perhaps the greatest artistic achievements of the period. Without them little would be known of Carolingian painting and sculpture. Book covers were frequently carved in ivory or cast in precious metal. The *Codex Aureus* of St. Emmeram and the *Lindau Gospels Cover* are the best examples. ■

Charlemagne's Royal Palace Chapel in Aachen, Germany, is the most impressive structure that survives from the Carolingian period. Illuminated manuscripts, ivory carvings, gold and silver reliefs on book covers and religious reliquaries have also survived in the monasteries and abbeys of Reims, Tours and St. Denis in France.

When Charlemagne died in 814, Europe was left open again to barbarian invasion and internal strife. In 936, the eastern Franks and the Saxons united to choose Otto I of Saxony (912–73) to be their king. Otto I was crowned Holy Roman Emperor by Pope John XII in 962. He reestablished imperial rule in Italy. Otto I successfully continued Charlemagne's policy of cultural revival by supporting building projects and the Church's role of educating artists. The Church was responsible for the advancement of writing through the development of books and illuminated manuscripts. Latin became the common language for all written works. Bishops were powerful figures because they could make decisions about construction of buildings and creation of works of art so they controlled the political and cultural life of the religious communities.

Ottonian art absorbed Byzantine taste in painting and relief carving. Celtic animals, monsters and plant images, in a great variety of abstract themes, were used in carved capitals in churches. Germanic art began to express the emotions of the artist, and this search for inner experiences was a revolutionary break with earlier traditions. Objects of religious significance, such as portable altars and freestanding holy images, were given an important place in Ottonian art.

Adam and Eve are ▶ *reproached in this detail from the bronze doors commissioned for Hildesheim Cathedral, completed in 1015. The artist used the open Ottonian style.*

6 Art of the Norsemen, the Normans and the Anglo-Saxons

Normandy

The Norsemen who came to the area known as Normandy after 911, radically changed the character and structure of the society there. Many farmers came from Scandinavia to Normandy to work the land that had once belonged to a few feudal lords. During the tenth century, Normandy extended its territory. The pagan custom of having more than one wife was common and lasted until the area was Christianized. ■

▲ The Annunciation *from the* Benedictional of St. Aethelwold, *made between 975 and 980 is a masterpiece of English illuminated manuscripts.*

The Norsemen raided the coasts of Europe, Ireland and Great Britain from the end of eighth century and later invaded northern France and Germany. The Norsemen spoke a Germanic language. Through contact with the Christianized Saxons and Franks they slowly came to know about Christianity. They occupied and settled in northern France at the beginning of the tenth century. In 911, the Frankish King Charles the Simple granted land, later known as the Duchy of Normandy, to Rollo, a Norse ruler. The Norsemen in the region came to be called Normans. They soon adopted Christianity and the Carolingian civilization.

The Viking invasions of England throughout the ninth century had disrupted cultural life, but after 959, when Anglo-Saxon and Danish territories had been agreed, there was relative stability in England under Anglo-Saxon kings. Inspired by the figures of St. Dunstan, archbishop of Canterbury from 958 to 988, St. Oswald, archbishop of York from 972 to 992 and St. Aethelwold, bishop of Winchester from 963 to 984, new monasteries were founded. Artistic expression, particularly in the form of illuminated manuscripts, assumed great importance. In this period, English architecture was largely influenced by the Carolingian style.

Between the ninth and tenth centuries, the cultural center of England moved from the north to the Saxon kingdom of Wessex, in the southwest. By the year 1000, illuminated manuscripts were being produced showing Viking animal ornamentation and an Irish writing style.

Illuminated manuscripts reflect the best achievements in Anglo-Saxon art in the ninth, tenth and eleventh centuries. Manuscripts produced in the scriptoria of Winchester, the capital, were more similar to the continental style than those examples found in Ireland and Northumbria. *The Annunciation* from the *Benedictional of St. Aethewold*, produced about 980, is an example of the work produced in Winchester. It certainly could compete with the finest Ottonian period manuscripts.

Irish-influenced stone work continued in the eleventh century. The Saxon custom was to erect stone crosses, often in a place where no church was located nearby for worship. The crosses were locations for everyday services of prayer. These crosses show the great competence and fine skill of the sculptors. They were an important artistic contribution.

The Bayeux Tapestry

Tapestries often documented great historic events and gave a clear representation of them. The Bayeux Tapestry illustrates the battle of Hastings. It was made to decorate the new Bayeux Cathedral in Normandy, consecrated in 1077, and was made in the style of the Canterbury school of embroidery. The story it tells concentrates on the main events and the detail of the embroidery makes the story clear. There is an accompanying text in Latin, but this type of tapestry was meant for an illiterate public. It consists of seventy-three panels, framed by ornamental decorations. It shows the conquest of England and scenes of daily life, such as ploughing and banquets of wild game. Women dressed in flowing garments are only represented in three panels . ∎

▲ The size of the Bayeux tapestry draws attention to its originality. The tapestry (1070–1080), embroidered in wool on linen, measures over 230 feet/69 meters in length. The scenes that tell the story of the bitter war between King Harold of England and Duke William of Normandy, which ended in 1066 with the Battle of Hastings, are clear, vivid and full of action. The composition leads on from one scene to the next. The figures have a naive look, but are very lively.

The Danish Viking kings, Sweyin and his son Canute, ruled England from 1013 to 1035 when the Anglo-Saxon monarchy weakened after 990. Through complicated inter-marriages among the Viking, Norman and Anglo-Saxon royal families, the throne passed to the Saxon King Harold. William, Duke of Normandy (1027–1087) also had a claim to the English throne. He defeated Harold at the Battle of Hastings in 1066. William the Conqueror was crowned king of England on Christmas day of 1066 in Winchester Cathedral.

The Norman Conquest is considered the beginning of the Middle Ages in Great Britain. Over the next two decades the Normans subdued the whole of England and gave it the political, spiritual and social organization which would last to the end of the Middle Ages. The Normans played an important role in forming the political and cultural future of western Europe in the eleventh century.

The Normans in Sicily

Sicily was fought over from the eighth to the eleventh century by Byzantines, Arabs and Normans. Due to the flow of people from different cultures the artistic styles that resulted show a blend of influences. Architecture was essentially Norman, while Arab decoration was maintained and wall mosaics showed Byzantine influence. Evidence of this can be found today in Palermo and Messina in Sicily. The Normans ruled Sicily between 1060 and 1194, providing economic stability and artistic development. Churches and palaces were built in great numbers. ∎

▲ The immense figure of Christ Pantocrator, is the main focus of the Byzantine mosaics that decorate the Cathedral of Monreale, built between 1166 and 1189.

7 Romanesque Art

In this French miniature of St. John Evangelist, *from the* Gospel Book of Abbot Wedricus *made about 1147, the Celtic-Germanic origins are evident. The decorative floral design and the figures in the spheres form part of the frame. The figure of the evangelist is represented by a strong, sweeping, linear curve, starting from the left foot and ending at the right ear. The elements of the design recall abstract Celtic decorations and show a strong Byzantine influence.*

The year 1000 brought to Europe a new and energetic spirit. After years of barbarian destruction, urban centers developed and commerce flowered. Economic, political and cultural development was stimulated.

Trade routes with the East were freed from continual Arab attacks at sea. The Italian navies of Genoa, Pisa and Venice now protected shipping. Europeans had goods to trade with the East for precious fabrics, oriental spices and jewelry. Renewed commerce within Europe led to the organization of trade guilds and the growth of villages. Uprisings against feudal lords by overtaxed subjects throughout Europe, together with the rise of a new middle class of merchants, led to great changes on the Continent.

The Church and its head, the pope, were the guiding and unifying forces in most people's lives. The monastic system, which had spread the spiritual teachings of the Church throughout Europe from the fifth century,

Reconstruction

At the end of the tenth century, architects faced technical difficulties, because building in stone had almost completely stopped over the previous 500 years. In Italy, architects studied ancient Roman architecture and rediscovered the building techniques they needed. Italian architects continued to build uninterruptedly during barbarian invasions, so they had not totally lost the techniques. In the eleventh century, they were asked to build churches throughout Europe. As a result there is a great similarity in buildings throughout Europe from this time. These churches had timbered roofs, round and square columns, plain block capitals and an air of simplicity. ■

▲ *Pisa cathedral, begun in 1174, has a special place in Italian Romanesque architecture, because of the harmonious relationship between the cathedral, baptistery and bell tower.*

▲ *Eleventh and twelfth century religious architecture in England shows the development of individual tastes. Architects tended to lengthen the nave. The high vaulted ceiling of Durham cathedral, built between 1093 and 1133, is characteristic.*

unleashed religious fervor everywhere.

In the eleventh century, there was a great burst of artistic energy throughout Europe and a new religious vision. As a result, there was a renewed need for painted and sculpted images, to replace those which had been destroyed by the iconoclasts and the barbarians over the previous 500 years. A vital and original artistic style came into being and appeared throughout Europe. This was the Romanesque style. Romanesque painting, illuminated manuscripts, sculptural decoration and architecture sprang from many sources. Roman, Celtic-Germanic, Carolingian and Ottonian styles were blended together.

The Romanesque style opened up space and gave greater height and size to buildings and introduced ribbed, vaulted roofs. High and low relief sculpture became a characteristic part of the decoration of the arcaded façades of buildings. There was a return to the Roman style and artists began to portray human figures in a naturalistic way.

Thousands of churches were built. Their decoration was richer and more splendid than any before. The Romanesque style did not follow strict new rules of design. It used models and imagery for architecture handed down from antiquity and showed strong, regional variations.

New stone sculptures began to appear again in about the year 1000 along the routes in southern France and northern Spain that pilgrims traveled on to holy places. These sculptures were monumental in size and were intended to impress and inspire the pilgrims.

Because of the earlier destruction of sculpture, medieval sculptors

▲ *The* Weighing of the Souls *in the tympanum of Cathedral Saint-Lazare in Autun, France, was made between 1130 and 1140 and was intended to strike fear into the hearts of viewers.*

Crusades and Pilgrimages

The most famous crusades were expeditions made by Christians to liberate the "Holy Land" from Islamic rule. Between the years 1096 and 1192, almost two million people, including women and children, from all over Europe, joined three crusades.

From the time of Constantine, Christians took part in pilgrimages to Christian holy places. By going on a pilgrimage, pilgrims could be forgiven for their sins and gain their souls' salvation after death. A pilgrimage meant leaving behind comfort and family, and required time, money and courage. Along the pilgrim routes new churches were built in great numbers. Movement of people through Europe, in pilgrimages and crusades, spread culture and art styles. ■

Painting in France and Spain

Many of the paintings produced in the eleventh century in France and Spain have been lost or fragmented. They were painted in tempera. Painting at this time followed Byzantine style or the linear arabesques of the art of barbarian invaders. The forms are simplified and stylized, very like the figures, plants and animals found in the sculptural reliefs of church façades. Figures are sharply outlined enclosing uniform areas of color, such as red, yellow and blue. Surviving examples of Romanesque French paintings can be seen in the church of St. Germain, Auxerre, in the baptistery of St. Jean, Poitiers, and in Puy Cathedral. In Spain, most paintings were reproduced in the north, closest to French influence, and along the pilgrim roads to Santiago de Compostela, far from menacing Arab invasion. Examples of these paintings are preserved in the Museum of Catalan Art at Barcelona. ■

had few models to copy. Artists had to depend on instinct to express their inner feelings and imagination and they had to develop their own language of expression for each medium. Sculptors and painters found their sources in Carolingian and Ottonian illuminated manuscripts, ivories and textiles. Allegorical themes began to appear alongside the traditional religious subjects.

The important subjects in sculpture and painting were religious. They were concerned with the end of the world and the last judgment, purgatory, damnation and salvation. Artists took great liberties in dealing with the human form, nature, spatial relations and color. They used their imaginations to represent fantastic grotesques, or unrealistic human forms, and highly stylized animal and plant life. Most sculptural decorations were made as parts of buildings, becoming capitals of columns or filling the arches of façades. They were used primarily for the capitals of the piers or for columns and portals of churches. They were sculpted in low relief. The results are highly individual and draw the viewer into the mysterious medieval world.

The human figure was given back weight and volume. Its feet were planted firmly on the ground. The body's humanity was emphasized by exaggerating heads, arms and legs. Once artists had abandoned the rigid, frontal pose of Byzantine work, figures became animated and charged with life. Sculpture developed mainly in France, Spain and Italy and each country manifested its own character.

The schools of Aquitaine and Burgundy, in France, were among the most important. Their work still maintained rigid frontal poses and can be seen today in the church of St. Sernin, Toulouse. The sculpture there

The decorative carvings in the church of ▶ La Madeleine in Vézeslay, France are rich in design ideas. The figures in this detail are of contrasting sizes and interact with animation in the sunburst framework in which they have been placed. The sculptor arranged the figures symmetrically to achieve a geometric composition, a reminder of Celtic-Germanic influences. The church was built between 1125 and 1130.

was made in 1096 by Bernard Gilduin, who found his source in late Roman sarcophagi.

Romanesque sculpture developed in northern Italy, for example, at St. Ambrogio, Milan, and in Emilia Romagna, a region of central Italy, particularly in Modena. Between 1099 and 1106 the artist Master Wiligelmo made the decorative sculpture for the façade of the cathedral of Modena.

French and Italian influences are found in Spanish sculpture which was intended to be free-standing or almost free-standing. The three-dimensional volume of this sculpture is clearly expressed in the figures of the apostles, in Oviedo Cathedral, in northern Spain. It can also be seen in the figures of prophets and apostles on the doors of the church at Santiago de Compostela produced by the sculptor Master Mateo in 1188.

In Germany, sculpture continued to be made in the Ottonian style. Original ideas are found in the bronze doors at Hildesheim Cathedral which are illustrated in chapter five.

The Ottonian style influenced English sculpture as seen in Chichester Cathedral, built between 1091 and 1123. The figures there have intense and dramatic expressions. Work in central and southern England shows French influences, for example in Lincoln Cathedral. Sculptures of the apostles at Malmesbury Abbey have a strong linear composition which draws the eye through the design and is dramatized by the rich drapery of the figures.

Urban Centers

Urban centers developed alongside church buildings during the Romanesque period. After the year 1000, walls were built around towns to protect them. An important aspect of domestic building in towns was the construction of towers, particularly in Italy. They were built in great numbers by noble families. The height of a tower signified the importance and power in the community of its owners. Florence and Bologna, in Italy, had 150 and 180 towers respectively, most of which were destroyed in the following centuries. ■

This is a detail of ▶ the Ascension from the tympanum on the façade of the church of Angoulême, Angoumois, France, begun in 1125. The powerful symmetry of its composition captures the viewer's attention. The viewer also feels the charged energy of the figures held within their architectural frames, for once the eye focuses on them they seem to visually spring to life.

8 Gothic Art

One of the finest examples of the French ▶ Gothic style is found in Chartres Cathedral. The Bishop of Chartres shared the ideas of his friend Abbot Sugar and began to rebuild his cathedral in the new style about 1145. When fire destroyed most of the building in 1150, rebuilding began again in 1194 and was completed in 1220. The cathedral still has most of its original stained glass. A visit to Chartres Cathedral is unforgetable because of the "miraculous" light of the windows.

Stained Glass

The dull light of northern Europe meant that large cathedrals required great openings in their walls to give sufficient light. Stained glass offered decoration as well as illumination. It had already been used in the Carolingian period and, in the Gothic period, stained glass appeared throughout France and Germany. The huge windows in the churches became an essential element of architecture. The technique united colored fragments of glass, which were cut to shape and set in lead straps. Drawings of details were made on the surface by using a fired, glazed brown color. Blues and reds, oranges and greens and brilliant white glass, set next to one another seem to float in their heavy, black, lead outlines. Biblical themes and the lives of the saints were represented. The viewer feels transported and detached from the real world in this array of colored and diffused light. The most important examples of stained glass windows are found in the twelfth century Chartres Cathedral, and in the Sainte Chapelle, Paris, built in the thirteenth century. ■

Man's energy was again fired into action in the middle of the twelfth century. A great change took place in medieval life. In the thirteenth century, Frederick II (1194–1250) became Holy Roman Emperor in 1212, and throughout his reign his forces and those of the pope were locked in struggles which led to their decline.

In Italy, steady economic growth became possible when the city-states were finally freed from imperial interference. The new middle classes created guilds to defend the interests of workers and began to exercise political influence. In the twelfth and thirteenth centuries, the guilds began to take a greater part in governing the city. Merchants began to trade across the whole of Europe. The cities of Genoa and Venice, in Italy, intensified maritime trade with ports throughout the Mediterranean and the Black Sea. In 1271, the Venetian explorer Marco Polo (1254–1324) left on an expedition to China, returning only in 1295. He opened new commercial, cultural, scientific and artistic horizons. The arts, in all their forms, began to thrive in a climate of civic and cultural enthusiasm.

The Gothic style that spread throughout Europe grew out of this

Sculpture in France underwent an ▶ *important change at the end of the twelfth century. The statues at the west portal of Chartres Cathedral of kings, queens, bishops and soldiers are separate entities from the columns, which recede into the shadow of the structure.*

Ribbed Vaulting ____

Ribbed vaulting was the most distinctive element of Gothic architecture. Stone vaults were built on the principal arches and joined by a framework of ribs to support the masonry above. This meant that the ceilings of churches could be raised much higher. ■

fertile atmosphere of exploration, questioning and experimentation. A desire for knowledge about the physical, natural and psychological worlds developed. Religious faith and the inner spiritual life were no longer enough for the curious medieval mind. A new attitude toward religion and toward the real world brought about the revolutionary

▲ *The pulpit of the baptistery at Pisa, executed in 1260, is Nicola Pisano's most masterful work, and clearly shows his interest in the works of antiquity. A surprising naturalism can be seen, and there is a tender human exchange between the figures.*

Gothic Sculpture _____

Sculpture in the round was revived in the twelfth century as decorative architectural elements. Early Gothic sculpture in France, from 1150 onward, was produced as decoration for cathedral façades. The best work is found on the façades of the cathedrals of Chartres and Amiens, in France. Here the sculptures had a clear design and sense of order. The sculptures on the portals of Chartres Cathedral break with the past, because they can be understood as free-standing statues, as well as an organic part of the architecture. The figures assume realistic and natural poses.

By the end of the twelfth century, more attention was given to the modeling of the body, textural surfaces, folds and drapery in sculpture. The sculpted image suddenly seemed to come to life for the first time since ancient Roman times.

In the late thirteenth century, the most perfect expression of Italian Gothic sculpture was achieved by three Italians, Nicola Pisano (approx. 1225–approx. 1284), Nicola's son Giovanni (approx. 1245–approx. 1320) and Arnolfo di Cambio (1232–1302). The body of work produced by these three artists clearly leads the way from the Romanesque tradition to the self-conscious art of the Gothic period. ■

The Madonna ▶ Enthroned, *was painted by Cimabue in the 1280s. Cimabue showed his mastery by endowing the figures with delicate human expressions. He achieved refined harmonies of color.*

Italian Influence

Illuminated manuscripts had undergone changes in the second half of the fourteenth century, inspired mainly by the great Italian painter Duccio. Duccio was known for his famous painting of the *Maestà* in Siena Cathedral. Landscape and deep space, first used by Duccio, were a revelation to northern artists and the influence of Duccio's work can be traced to the city of Prague, in the Czech Republic, which was a center of international culture. *Death of the Virgin*, painted between 1350 and 1360 by a painter known as the Bohemian Master and illustrated on page 28, is an excellent example showing Italian influence. ■

Giotto gave depth to his pictures. This had ▶ *not been done since Roman times. In the* Deposition of Christ, *a fresco painted about 1304 to 1313, Giotto produced a scene of human tragedy filled with emotion and showed his command of light, perspective and drama. He used the elements of the landscape to send the eye of the spectator across the scene and up to the dead tree. Agitated angels excite the atmosphere, contrasting with the group over the dead Christ.*

Perspective and Vanishing Points_

Perspective in painting and drawing is a mathematical plan for representing objects and distance on one plane as they appear to the eye. The spectator is given a single viewpoint called a vanishing point. It is a point on the horizon, fixed by the artist, where all lines from the picture plan converge. ■

changes found in Gothic art, and a new figurative art and architecture developed.

The Gothic style first appeared in France, in the rebuilding of the royal abbey church of St. Denis between 1137 and 1144. The new style spread from St. Denis to nearby Paris and the surrounding area. By 1250, most of Europe had adopted it. The new, French Gothic style changed slowly as it absorbed a variety of tastes and local differences.

In Italy, the Gothic style of architecture was essentially static. The Italians sought solidity and quiet harmony in their buildings, sculpture and paintings, while the French strove for energetic movement. In Germany, the Romanesque tradition persisted because of the influence of the Ottonian period, in spite of the acceptance of early French Gothic ideas and trends.

Gothic artists continued to represent nature using symbols and then found a place for symbols in their art by fusing sculpture harmonious-

The Plague

The population of Europe began to increase at the end of the eleventh century. By the middle of the fourteenth century a series of bad harvests led to famine and the population began to decline. In 1347 bubonic plague, or the Black Death, reached Europe from central Asia. The disease was carried by fleas which lived on rats carried on ships and overland caravans from the East. By 1350, Rome, Florence, Paris and London had felt the ravages of the plague and the consequences were staggering. A quarter of the population of Europe had died. Farmers could not cultivate their land for lack of labor, food production collapsed and commerce was paralyzed. Plague affected everyone, including artists. Many artists and craftsmen died or fled from infected urban centers and the arts were left in a state of isolation and decline. ■

ly with architecture. However, during the Middle Ages, as man's view of his place in the world underwent a transformation so, too, did art. By the late thirteenth century some artists began to represent nature realistically. They began to create a religious art filled with concrete images of the world and with emotional content.

In thirteenth century Italy, there was a special need for decoration in the great interior wall surfaces of the cathedrals. They were not filled with stained glass windows, as they were in northern Europe. They were perfect surfaces for fresco decoration. Cenni di Pepi, known as Cimabue (approx. 1240–approx. 1308) was the most prominent figure in Italian Gothic painting at the end of the thirteenth century. He produced some of the finest Gothic frescoes and mosaics. He was a great innovator and expressed, for the first time in the history of painting, a more direct relationship between the sacred image of Christ and real people in his work. Cimabue was not concerned with showing deep space in painting, but his development of the human figure was revolutionary.

One of the most important and exciting discoveries in Gothic painting was made by the Italian Duccio di Buoninsegna, from Siena, Italy, who was active between 1278 and 1319. Duccio invented a new pictorial space, which can be seen in his *Annunciation of the Death of the Virgin*, painted between 1308 and 1311. For the first time, Duccio surrounded two figures in a painting with an architectural interior.

The Italian painter Giotto, (approx. 1267–1336), understood and built on past traditions. He developed light and shading called

The Limbourg Brothers

The Flemish brothers Pol, Jan and Hermann Limbourg had settled in France at the court of the Duke of Berry by 1413. They illuminated the manuscript of *Les Très Riches Heures du Duc de Berry* for him. It is considered one of the best examples of medieval illuminated manuscripts using the International Gothic style. The work was actually a prayer book. The prayers were accompanied by a calendar and the months were illustrated with the season's activities. The Limbourg brothers observed in minute detail the different aspects of nature and man's life. Their calligraphic lines, intense vibrant colors and masterful use of aerial perspective, as if the scenes were viewed from above, characterized their artistic expression. By 1416, seventy-one miniatures had been painted. The deaths of the artists and of their patron prevented the work's completion. ■

◄ *The month of August is welcomed by the happy procession of courtly lovers riding to the hunt in one of the illustrations for* Les Très Riches Heures du Duc de Berry, *painted by the Limbourg brothers between 1413 and 1416.*

▲ Death of the Virgin, *painted between 1350 and 1360 by the Bohemian Master, shows the Italian influence of painters like Duccio.*

The northern painters, such as Robert Campin (active 1406–44), brought the scenes depicted in their paintings down to earth. The careful details of Campin's Nativity *painted about 1425 records details from life in the fifteenth century.* ▼

chiaroscuro, in fresco painting. He was more successful than those artists before him in defining perspective and creating the illusion of space. He placed his subjects in realistic settings and architectural environments, and gave his figures individual character. Giotto made it possible for the viewer to clearly understand the actions of his figures and their exact location in the composition.

In the north, particularly in Flanders, a growing, thriving middle class forced Gothic art to fit the tastes and values of its increasing prosperity at the beginning of the fifteenth century. For the first time, art was used not only for religious purposes, but also to portray the wealth and status of prominent citizens. Cotton merchants who benefited from the expanding trade with the East were the new patrons of the arts. These wealthy patrons required an art that reflected the reality of their world, while Gothic portraits depicted human emotion and a vision of life which is artificial and idealized. A sudden change of style took place nearly everywhere in Europe, as the International Gothic style made its appearance in response to the demands of the new middle class.

One of the important features of the International Gothic style in painting is a concern with detail. Artists projected their sharp, exact observation into deep space. The landscape was treated as a backdrop or a theatrical set. The vigorous sweep of the Gothic movement of line, in the flowing mantles worn by the figures, was made to seem more voluminous by the use of light and shade. Figures with harmonious proportions now stood solidly on the ground and assumed natural poses in new works of art.

Rogier van der Weyden, (1400–64), the student of Robert Campin, tried to express dramatic emotion in his work. The viewer is struck by the limited space in the foreground where the action takes place. This suggests that the artist may have been inspired by early Gothic sculptures found in the niches of cathedrals. ▶

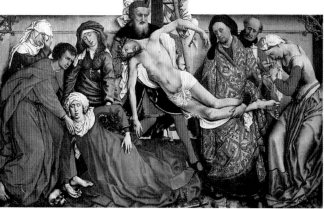

9 Early Renaissance Art

▲ *Ghiberti's 1401 competition piece for the bronze doors of the Baptistery at Florence,* The Sacrifice of Isaac, *is closer to the International Gothic style, than the Renaissance style.*

Donatello's ▶ David, made early in his career between 1430 and 1432, is the first Renaissance free-standing bronze which imitates living flesh. The brooding aspect of the figure and its dramatic effect are characteristic of Donatello's work.

In the fifteenth and sixteenth centuries there was a great change in attitude called the Renaissance, meaning a rebirth. Human spirit and reason became all-important. A new vision of life led to freedom of thought, the development of the individual, curiosity about the human race and the world, scientific research, inventions, travel and discovery.

In the Renaissance, art, literature, music and mathematics were considered the highest spiritual achievements of man. Artists gained a new status. They exercised great influence on people's lives and thinking. They became instrumental in forming the social, cultural and intellectual life of the community.

In the fourteenth century, patronage of the arts had moved from the religious authorities and aristocratic nobility to the rising middle class of merchants, bankers and contractors. They now commissioned buildings and works of art. They were responsible for circulating works of art and spreading foreign artistic ideas throughout Europe.

At the opening of the fifteenth century, the city of Florence, Italy, had a democratic government. It was one of the richest cities in Europe. The Florentine cloth finishing industry was known throughout Europe and its banking system was the most stable in the world. Above all, Florence was populated by a great number of the most talented artists in Europe. It flourished throughout the century under the benevolent, though stern, rule of the Medici family.

In 1400, the Florentines had decided to complete two major pro-

The Medici Family_____

The history of the rich Florentine Medici family dates back to 1251. Their immense wealth was created by lending money to the most important Italian families. Cosimo the Old (1389–1464), known as "the Father of the Country," governed Florence from 1429 until his death. He established commercial relationships with the whole of Europe and with the East. In 1436, Cosimo brought about a balance of power among the five major Italian city-states of Florence, Venice, Milan, Rome and Naples, and assured a period of peace. He encouraged and protected the arts. Cosimo's grandson, Lorenzo the Magnificent (1449–92), continued his grandfather's policies and governed Florence from 1469 to his death. Lorenzo, a poet and a writer himself, was patron to the major artists of his time. ■

Palaces

Early Renaissance Florentine palace designs were derived from the ancient Roman houses at Ostia, near Rome. The Palazzo Davanzati is a fine example. The palace had five stories, including the loggia. The ground floor was used as a warehouse. The second floor contained reception rooms and the adults' sleeping quarters. The third floor was for the children. The fourth, high up under the roof, was used by the servants, since it was hot there in summer and cold in winter. The loggia, on the roof, was used for drying laundry, and the family would take the air there in the hot summer. Renaissance palaces were symmetrical, built around an inner court. Their general appearance is sober and severe. The structures give an imposing and striking sense of permanence, like fortresses. ■

▲ *The figures in Nanni di Banco's* Four Saints *were made in marble between about 1410 to 1414. They are approximately lifesize, they are portrayed realistically and stand solidly on the ground. Several of the figures even appear to express emotion in their faces.*

Masaccio's understanding of individual ▶ *human character, captured in the head of Christ and the apostles in the fresco* The Tribute Money, *of 1427, is combined with Giotto's spatial grandeur. The artist reproduced three episodes in the same picture and presented landscape convincingly for the first time in western painting.*

jects started in the previous century: the great bronze doors of the baptistery and the decoration of the façade of the cathedral. The completion of the baptistery doors represented the symbolic opening of the Renaissance in Europe. The competition for the commission was won by Lorenzo Ghiberti (1378–1455). His 1401 entry, *The Sacrifice of Isaac*, set the Early Renaissance in motion. It created a bridge between the Gothic and Renaissance styles, with its linear, sweeping Gothic movement and classical Renaissance proportions.

Donatello (1386–1466) is considered the greatest sculptor of the Early Renaissance. His sculptures of St. Mark and St. George, executed between 1411 and 1416 for the church of Or San Michele in Florence were influenced by the Gothic style. The classical pose of the figures is hidden by the voluminous robes, but the forms are massive and solid. *The Annunciation* in Santa Croce, completed in 1408 in limestone, is a high relief. Donatello introduced a completely new way of representing a religious event in sculpture, by placing an episode from the New Testament in a contemporary setting.

The sculptor Nanni di Banco (approx. 1384–1421) found his inspiration in classical Roman art where he rediscovered its realism. He emphasized the classical proportions of the human figure. *Four Saints*, made between 1410 and 1414, in Or San Michele, could be four figures taken directly from the Arch of Constantine in Rome, built 1100 years earlier. The folds of their mantles accentuate the figures' relaxed

Strong perspective forces the viewer to ▶ accept the realism of this portion of The Discovery and Proving of the True Cross of about 1460 by Piero della Francesca. However, stark triangles, circles, rectangles and squares lead the viewer into an abstract world.

Filippo Brunelleschi _

The sculptor-architect Filippo Brunelleschi (1377–1446) traveled to Rome with the sculptor Donatello on several occasions, to study the ancient ruins. They wanted to learn how the Romans represented the human figure and to study Roman buildings. Brunelleschi was convinced that the Romans used a system of measurement which ensured perfect proportions and beautiful harmony in buildings. The Foundling Hospital in Florence, designed by Brunelleschi between 1419 and 1424 is thought to be the earliest Renaissance building. He was commissioned by the Medici family to build the first Renaissance church, St. Lorenzo, in 1419. Brunelleschi's major achievement was the design and construction of the dome spanning the huge space in St. Maria dei Fiori, in Florence. ■

The beautiful loggia which runs along the front of Brunelleschi's Foundling Hospital in Florence, Italy, is reminiscent of Romanesque cloisters, because of the scale of the colonnade and the number of arches. The straightforwardness of its elegant design prepared the way for buildings of the Early Renaissance. ▼

classical poses. The heads are very similar to Roman ones in their realism.

Early Renaissance painting was born of the efforts of one man: Masaccio (1401–28). Masaccio understood the changes in sculpture and architecture in his time and transferred the new ideas to his painting. He resolved the problems of modeling three-dimensional form, deep space, chiaroscuro and the representation of human drama in his work. For the first time in western painting, landscape settings receded convincingly into the distance. Masaccio took Giotto's lesson in modeling human forms and made them more believable. He defined the relationship of the human figure to the environment in mathematical terms.

Piero della Francesca (approx. 1416–92) continued to paint monumental frescoes in the manner of Giotto and Masaccio. His most ambitious work, the frescoes for the church of St. Francesco, in Arezzo, Italy, completed between about 1452 and 1459, cast a different light on Early Renaissance perceptions of the world. His figures seem to be in a state of suspended animation where all movement has stopped.

The paintings of Andrea del Castagno (1423–57) are an excellent contrast to Piero della Francesca's frescoes. His figures in *The Last Supper*, of 1445 to 1450, in the monastery of St. Apollonia, Florence, seem to reject the rigid and severely decorative interior. The vigorous and agitated lines and forms of the robes, caught in contrasting light and dark, and the expressiveness of the faces reveal an energy about to be released. The squares of the decorated walls above seem to bear down on the seated figures, creating tension in the entire composition.

Andrea del Castagno established the focus of ▶ *his fresco,* The Last Supper, *painted between 1445 and 1459, through the veining of the decorative marble above the heads of his main characters which looks like a bolt of lightning.*

Anatomy

Their attraction to antique art inevitably led curious Renaissance artists to study the classical nude figure, found mainly in relief sculpture on Roman sarcophagi. It was not until the sixteenth century that artists began to explore human anatomy by examining and dissecting cadavers. Leonardo da Vinci and Michelangelo made the first such studies in anatomy. Ultimately they redirected the entire course of study of the human nude in western art. Antonio del Pollaiuolo (approx. 1431–98), a painter, engraver and sculptor, more than any other artist of the Early Renaissance, resolved the problem of the nude in action. There is a close relationship in his work to the figures found in the vase paintings of ancient Greece. Muscular definition and modeled form are revealed in his work by portraying the nude under stress. ■

Three painters dominated the second half of the Early Renaissance. They were Perugino (approx. 1450–1523), Luca Signorelli (approx. 1441–1523), and Sandro Botticelli (1445–1510). All three artists worked on the completion of the first fresco cycles in the Sistine Chapel in Rome, the major artistic achievement in Italy during this period of the Renaissance.

Perugino had probably learned to paint in oils under the Florentine sculptor and painter Andrea del Verrocchio (approx. 1435–88). Perugino's achievements are his spatial clarity and the grace he gave to his figures. He was commissioned in 1482 to work on the fresco cycles at the Sistine Chapel. His *Charge to Peter* is the most outstanding work of the period.

Luca Signorelli was concerned with the study of anatomy and antiquity. In 1482, he, too, was called to Rome to work on the Sistine frescoes. His outstanding works are the *Flagellation*, of about 1475, now in Brera Museum, Milan, and the *Last Judgment* frescoes, of 1499 to 1504, in Orvieto Cathedral, Italy.

Sandro Botticelli was an excellent draughtsman. The cool detachment of his figures shows both classical and Gothic influences. His highest achievements are figures that are graceful, languid and melan-

Botticelli's The Birth of Venus, *painted* ▶ *about 1480 in tempera on canvas, brings to a climax the art of the Early Renaissance. In the depiction of the most celebrated nude of the Renaissance, the artist courageously confronts two major art influences of his time: the emotional impact of dramatic movement obtained by using the grand sweep of lines of a Gothic composition and a Renaissance desire to exalt the beauty of the human form. The composition is original and a masterpiece of pictorial achievement, bringing together classical ideals and rendering them in a modern way.*

The horsemen in the foreground of ▶
The Battle of San Romano, *tempera and silver foil on wood of about 1455 by Paolo Uccello, have the appearance of stuffed figures suspended in action. Uccello's early training in the International Gothic style is evident in the dominating sweep of lines. His late works tend to be closer to the Renaissance ideal.*

Mantegna's St. Sebastian *painted in tempera about 1455 to 1460, is full of information about antiquity. The saint is part of the architectural ruins. The artist directs the viewer's eyes from the world of antiquity found in the foreground to a strange mixture of present and past in the middle and background.* ▼

cholic. The subjects of his paintings are often set in unrealistic and highly detailed environments.

In northern Italy, the Renaissance style did not appear until the middle of the fifteenth century when Venice became its northern center. Venice, a flourishing republic, had close connections with Florence. Florentine artists were commissioned to create works in Venice. Donatello, Paolo Uccello, Andrea del Castagno and Fra' Filippo Lippi had worked in Venice. Andrea Mantegna (1431–1506) began the Venetian Renaissance. His works continued the tradition of Masaccio, by reproducing the architecture of antiquity in precise, perspective planes. His human figures show intense emotions.

Mantegna's brother-in-law Giovanni Bellini (approx. 1431–1516) was an important northern Italian painter. Bellini became interested in northern Gothic painting around 1475. Soon after he had mastered the technique of oil painting, his work became texturally more sensual with warm, vibrant colors. He brought landscape painting to a high level of development.

While Italy was caught in the powerful grip of Early Renaissance art, intellectual thought and discoveries, most of the rest of Europe was still producing painting, sculpture and graphic arts in the Gothic style.

Luca della Robbia

After Donatello, the most significant sculptor in Florence in the first half of the Early Renaissance was Luca della Robbia (1400–1482). His major works were made in terracotta or fired earthenware. His figures reflect some of Ghiberti's style, with overtones of classical Roman reliefs. Della Robbia's art characteristically has a gentle sweetness and a serene and sober dignity. White glazed figures suggesting marble, placed against deep blue backgrounds, are typical of della Robbia's reliefs. ■

10 High Renaissance Art in Italy

▲ *Leonardo da Vinci's fresco* The Last Supper, *of 1495 to 1498, is often described as the first painting of the High Renaissance.*

The sixteenth century was the most important period in Italian art. Artistic contributions made since the time of the Romans bore fruit in the work of the geniuses who dominated the period. The Early Renaissance was primarily an Italian phenomenon in art, but the High Renaissance style took hold throughout Europe. It began in Italy at the end of the fifteenth and the beginning of the sixteenth centuries for several reasons. Italians were the social and economic leaders of Europe. The first European banking system was developed in Italy. The urban middle class had political power and social standing in Italy earlier than elsewhere. The idea of free commercial competition first took root in Italy. The art of classical antiquity was readily available to study there since more of it had been preserved in Italy. As a result, High Renaissance art came to portray a rich, powerful, culturally developed social class.

The fifteenth century artist was required to possess great versatility. Patrons demanded intelligence, self-assurance, broad scholarly and scientific knowledge and an aggressive, tenacious spirit. Artists of this period set high standards for themselves and the great personalities of the High Renaissance gave the world almost superhuman works of art.

Artists of the High Renaissance abandoned the logic and laws behind art of the Early Renaissance for a language that involved the observer's emotions. Each work was considered unique and not intended to be a building block for a new style. Few minor artists of the High Renaissance have stood the test of time, but the six major masters were Leonardo, Raphael, Michelangelo, Bramante, Giorgione and Titian. Their work influenced culture throughout Europe and

The composition of the figures and the sweet refinement of the Virgin and the angel in Leonardo da Vinci's The Virgin of the Rocks, *of about 1485, belong to Early Renaissance ideals.* ▼

Giorgione

Giorgione (approx. 1478–1510), rose like a comet in the Italian Renaissance. He has been called the founder of the Venetian High Renaissance, though in the thirty-two years that he lived, he produced few mature works. His early works were strongly influenced by the classical serenity and richness of color of his teacher Giovanni Bellini. Giorgione's late works, such as his portraits, are paintings of faces emerging from deep shadow, partially illuminated. ■

Giorgione's 1508 oil on canvas, The Tempest, *presents the world of* ▶ *nature, the cycle of life and the poet and dreamer, in a sensuous environment of color, light and impending storm. The disconnected images of the woman suckling her child, the standing youth gazing off, and the fragments of antiquity create a dreamy and romantic picture of escape.*

Donato Bramante was the inventor of the High Renaissance style of architecture. The Tempietto, *built in Rome in 1502, is the building by Bramante that most completely sums up the new architectural style. Inspired by classical temple architecture, its molded exterior is balanced by the little dome on top. Although the building is quite small in size, it has a monumental weight and balance.* ▼

overshadowed the work of the greatest artists for the next 300 years.

Early Renaissance artists did away with the Medieval and Gothic idea of rendering all parts of a picture precisely and in detail. They strove for a unity of all the parts of a painting. For High Renaissance artists unified proportion and space, a single theme and a clear composition that could be understood immediately by the viewer were the most important elements of a work of art.

Leonardo da Vinci (1452–1519) divided his energies between science, art and documenting his discoveries. More than anyone else in his time, he embodied the ideal of the universal man. He was educated in the arts and science and in tune with the latest human endeavors. In *The Last Supper*, Leonardo expressed both the aspirations, ideals and lessons of the Early Renaissance, and the advances in painting of the next two decades.

The titanic figure of Michelangelo Buonarroti (1475–1564) grasped

Donato Bramante

Donato Bramante (1444–1514) was the most important architect of the High Renaissance. He began life as a painter under the influence of Piero della Francesca and Mantegna. Leonardo's research into architecture influenced Bramante's architectural drawings of churches. In turn, Bramante's influence led to changes in Raphael's paintings, particularly in *The School of Athens*, a fresco at the Vatican. Bramante's *Tempietto*, built in Rome in 1502, to mark the site of St. Peter's crucifixion, was one of the early achievements in architecture that helped make Rome the center of Italian art during the early sixteenth century. ■

the raw material the universe offers. He touched the deep, primordial soul of man, breathing new life into it. More than any other High Renaissance master, he and his art embody the extraordinary drama, spirit and power of the age. His life and work demonstrate that unity which was the Renaissance goal. His art shows an immense flow of creative energy sustained throughout a career of seventy years. It embraced many forms of artistic expression: painting, sculpture and architecture.

After a short apprenticeship in 1488, with the Florentine painter Domenico Ghirlandaio (approx. 1448–94), Michelangelo joined the circle of artists under Lorenzo de' Medici's patronage. He devoted most

The Sistine Chapel

Sixtus IV (1414–84), who was pope from 1471 until his death, commissioned the Sistine Chapel at the Vatican in Rome. Its walls were decorated with frescoes produced by the major artists of the Early Renaissance. In 1508, Pope Julius II (1443–1513) commissioned Michelangelo to decorate the great ceiling of the chapel. In only four years he completed one of the major works in the history of art. He worked on his back on scaffolding, looking up at the ceiling. With incredible richness of imagination, he told the stories of Moses, Noah and Christ, accompanied by gigantic figures of the prophets and the sibyls who announce the coming of Christ and the creation of Adam. The entire ceiling is crowded with extraordinary figures revealing Michelangelo's mastery of the portrayal of man in all his human, emotional and psychological possibilities. Nearly thirty years later, Michelangelo also painted the *Last Judgment* on the wall above the altar. ■

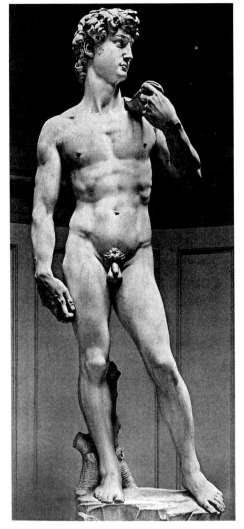

▲ *At the age of twenty-six, Michelangelo began his monumental statue of* David. *Michelangelo succeeded in giving his figure deep emotional and psychological weight, adding to its heroic physical presence.*

Michelangelo began work on the frescoes ▶ *for the Sistine Chapel ceiling in 1508 and completed the extraordinary work in just four years. The ceiling contains hundreds of figures that seem to move energetically within the architectural framework. Despite its monumental size, the work has a great sense of unity. This is* The Fall of Man and Expulsion from the Garden, *from the Sistine Chapel. Michelangelo's figures show the depth of feeling the artist had for his subject matter.*

Michelangelo ▶ demonstrated his capacity to unite architecture and sculpture in the reclining figures, Day and Night, designed so their poses lead the eye up to the seated figure, Giuliano de' Medici.

Titian

Titian (approx. 1487–1576) is considered one of the greatest High Renaissance painters. He remained faithful to the classical values of the Early Renaissance. He used lush, glowing color schemes as well as somber ones. He was a master at painting joyous themes. After 1540, he made more generous use of brushstrokes and his colors became darker while his forms were softened. ■

of his energy to sculpture and architecture. He demonstrated his great capacity for painting in Pope Julius II's commission for the Sistine Chapel. The nude was the expression which most suited Michelangelo. The human form in his work registered the course of his tumultuous life, filled both with great inspiration and profound disillusion.

The third pillar of the High Renaissance was Raphael (1483–1520). His formal education took place in the Umbrian master Perugino's studio. Raphael absorbed the calm, gentle spirit of the Umbrian region and of Perugino's painting so deeply that it stayed in his thinking and work for the rest of his thirty-seven years. He had a brilliant mind, capable of combining the formidable qualities of the works of Leonardo, Michelangelo and the last Renaissance architect, Bramante, in his own work. This capacity to unite the highest achievements of the period in his work makes Raphael the leading painter of the High Renaissance.

Raphael was commissioned to make almost every form of art and architecture. He was able to complete his many commissions by directing his studio of disciplined artists who were trained to produce to his high standard. His study of antique remains is evident in his frescoes of the *Triumph of Galatea* in the Villa Farnesina, Rome, made in about 1512. This research made him change the way he painted. He began to use monumental scale and painted figures in flowing drapery in mythological or allegorical settings. He used a refined, subtle and harmonious color range which he had found in antique frescoes and mosaics. One of his important innovations was dramatic chiaroscuro.

Raphael's grand fresco The School of Athens, *of 1510 to 1511, is often considered the artist's masterpiece because it represents the classical aspirations of the High Renaissance better than other works of art. The painting is divided in half horizontally. The upper part is devoted to architecture and the lower to the protagonists. ▼*

The story from Greek ▶ mythology of Galatea Pursued by Polyphemus, is a monumental fresco painted by Raphael in 1513. It is charged with sensuality. The painting demonstrates Raphael's control over classical principles of painting and his inclination to invent new pictorial settings.

11 Renaissance Art in Northern Europe

In Holland, Belgium and the rest of northern Europe, the late Gothic style still held sway during the fifteenth century. It was then that the Flemish School brought Gothic painting to its height. Flemish artists developed the new technique of painting in oils to improve the luminosity and transparency of their colors, giving sharpness to their images. The major contributions of the Flemish school are in portraiture, in defining interior settings and in landscapes.

Northern subject matter retained a medieval symbolism and religious abstraction. Greater liberties were taken in dealing with nature, animal and plant life and the human figure. Although it was central to the subjects of Flemish paintings, the human figure continued to have symbolic meaning. Sacred figures assumed unrealistic proportions. Naked human forms were often shown burdened with guilt.

Changes in northern art came about in the sixteenth century, when artists began to travel more frequently to Italy. They assimilated the discoveries of the Italian Renaissance, making change inevitable. The lessons brought home included the principles of perspective, concepts of architectural space and the return to classical proportions for the human figure.

The Protestant Reformation of religion started in Germany at the beginning of the

▲ Giovanni Arnolfini and His Wife, *by Jan van Eyck, 1434, is an early example of Flemish portraiture and the depiction of the interior of a middle class house. Interiors became a favorite theme of the Flemish school.*

The Effect of the Reformation

The Reformation brought a great crisis to painting. Painting began to disappear in northern Europe and England and for a time portraiture was all that survived. Paintings were no longer required for churches, but Flemish artists found a way around the problem. Their long tradition of the perfect imitation of nature allowed some Flemish painters to find a commercial outlet for their art with scenes of everyday life. This was the beginning of genre painting. Pieter Bruegel the Elder was the great master of genre painting, and specialized in rural and farm scenes. ■

Hieronymus Bosch

Hieronymus Bosch (1450–1516) has a unique place in Northern Renaissance painting. His great body of work documented the time and covers art, culture, religion and society. Bosch belonged to a religious brotherhood in his native town of Hertogenbosch, in the Low Countries. He was preoccupied with the medieval ideas of the opposition of good and evil, God and the devil. He felt that man had a choice between religion and the pleasures of this life. This conflict was common in northern European culture and often showed itself as fear and obsession in works of art, like Bosch's wonderful fantasies. ■

▲ *Hieronymus Bosch's oil painting technique was of the finest quality.* The Garden of Delights, *painted between 1510 and 1515, is a feast of fantastic imagery and a mixture of the normal and the grotesque. This detail from the central panel seems to tell of the folly of man as he plays the mad, enigmatic fool. The true meaning of Bosch's painting remains a mystery.*

Erasmus

Desiderius Erasmus (approx. 1466–1536) was a Christian humanist thinker and writer from Rotterdam who influenced thinking all over Europe. Erasmus wrote in Latin so his books could be read by educated men. While he remained in the Catholic Church, he criticized almost everyone and everything: popes, kings, institutions, wars, religion and scholars. His satires encouraged people to think and question everything. ■

sixteenth century. It came about for religious, economic and cultural reasons. The important figures at the beginning of the Reformation were Martin Luther in Germany, Desiderius Erasmus in the Low Countries (now the Netherlands and Belgium), Huldreich Zwingli and John Calvin in Switzerland, John Colet and Thomas Cranmer in England, all of whom understood the need for religious reform. Some of these men broke away from the Roman Catholic church and were called Protestants.

Many Protestants disapproved of carved and painted images because they, like the iconoclasts of ancient times, thought them idolatrous. Extremist Protestants destroyed churches, palaces, public buildings and all the religious imagery they could find. Martin Luther, the brilliant mind that inspired the Reformation in the hearts of common people, had not intended it to be used as a weapon of destruction. He was firmly against the indiscriminate annihilation of religious art. However, before the end of the sixteenth century, most of northern Europe felt the terrible consequences. Germany, Switzerland, England and part of France had all lost much of their artistic heritage.

In the sixteenth century, the Low Countries were part of the Hapsburg empire ruled by the Holy Roman Emperor Charles V, who was also king of Spain, and later ruled by Philip II of Spain. The Reformation led to conflict between the Low Countries and the Catholic Hapsburgs as they tried to suppress Protestantism. After bitter and bloody revolts, the northern provinces, which are today the Netherlands, won their independence, while Flanders in the south, now part of Belgium, remained under Spanish rule.

Despite the disruption of war between 1550 and 1600, most of the important artists in northern Europe came from the Low Countries. They laid the foundation for the great artistic works of the Flemish and Dutch masters in the next hundred years. Pieter Bruegel the Elder (approx. 1525–69), a painter and draftsman, was the outstanding Dutch artist. From what is known of him, he avoided the political and religious turmoil of his time.

▲ *The simple peasant life is given nobility in the scene of* The Peasant Wedding, *painted in oil by Pieter Bruegel the Elder in 1565.*

The Adam and Eve panels from van Eyck's Ghent Altarpiece, of 1432, have a special place in the history of painting. They are the earliest monumental nudes (almost life size) from the north of Europe. They were painted with a daring realism and scale which was quite new for religious paintings. ▼

The first important Flemish master was Jan van Eyck (approx. 1380–1441). Van Eyck began his career as an illuminator of manuscripts. He worked at the court of John of Bavaria, Count of Holland, at the Hague in 1422. In 1432, he was at work in Bruges, and produced his masterpiece for the cathedral, the *Polyptich with the Lamb*. The sacred subject is set in a lush green landscape, with Gothic-style buildings appearing on the horizon. The landscape, represented in minute detail, is the real subject. Depth is obtained by painting the

Oil Painting

Before the fifteenth century, colors were extracted from plants or made from ground up minerals. The powder obtained was made into a paste by mixing it with egg, a technique called egg tempera. Tempera did not give many different color tones or rich colors. It dried rapidly, forcing the artist to work hastily. Jan van Eyck, among others, realized that it was possible to use oil, which dried more slowly, in place of egg when mixing his colors. This allowed him to work more slowly and carefully. He could obtain brilliant colors by superimposing one on another. ■

receding fields, woods and mountains, in different tones of green leading to a distant haze on the horizon. The laws of perspective, however, are not followed. The figures are composed as if they are seen from the air, a characteristic of Gothic art. They are modeled with rounded form and dressed in rich robes and the details focus on their faces and precious jewelry.

At the end of the fifteenth century, there was a brief period of artistic achievement in Germany with the work of Albrecht Dürer, and Mathias Grünewald. Indeed, the Northern Renaissance can best be understood through the life and art of Albrecht Dürer (1471–1528) who was born

The figures of the ▶ *center panel of Grünewald's* Isenheim Altarpiece, *of about 1510 to 1515, painted in oil on wood, make a great impact on the viewer. Each figure fills its own space. The dark background heightens the drama of the tragic picture.*

▲ *The portrait of* Henry VIII, *painted in 1540 in oil by Hans Holbein the Younger, displays his skill at capturing the likeness and character of his subject.*

Printing Books

From the early fifteenth century the first books were printed from woodcuts. The invention of printing presses with movable type, in 1444, by the German Johannes Gutenberg (1400–68), meant that it was now possible to produce many copies of a book very cheaply. ■

in Nuremberg, Germany. He had a genius's intellectual power, sensitivity and capacity for invention. His achievements included painting, drawing and engraving. Coming from the Gothic tradition, he had a natural inclination toward drawing.

Dürer's art represents the dual forces of religious spirituality and naturalism. Dürer was a devout Christian who drew inspiration from his spirituality. He was also deeply interested in nature and accepted it for its own sake. Dürer was able to mold these two attitudes toward life together to produce his extraordinary and strange works. He was one of the many northern artists who traveled to Italy, seeking inspiration from the latest developments. He was attracted to Mantegna's drawings and Pollaiuolo's engravings.

Dürer's *The Apocalypse* was the first book written and illustrated by one artist. Dürer believed that artists must not lose their spontaneity. *The Apocalypse*, made demands on the engraver. Nevertheless, Dürer gave a fresh style and a brilliant technique full of precise and accurate detail to the woodcut illustrations. *The Four Horsemen*, of 1498, is the best known of these woodcuts. Dürer was capable of working out his thoughts with great speed and inventiveness, when cutting in wood or engraving metal, and the classical forms of his figures are defined with an intense and expressive line.

Italian Renaissance influences reached France earlier than other northern countries. Artists there combined the Renaissance style with local ideas and tastes. Jean Goujon (approx. 1510–68) was the most outstanding French sculptor of the mid-sixteenth century. His relief sculptures from the *Fountain of the Innocents*, made between 1547 and 1549, show the influence of Florentine sculpture.

In Albrecht ▶ *Dürer's engraving* Knight, Death and Evil, *produced in 1513, the knight represents a Christian soldier on the road to Jerusalem.*

The power of love is ▶ *the subject of Hans Baldung Grien's (approx. 1484–1545) first known drawing,* Aristotle and Phyllis. *Dürer's influence is evident in the clarity of the forms, particularly in the figures and the folds of their clothes.*

12 Mannerist Art

In his representation of The Burial of Count ▶
Orgaz, *painted in oil on canvas in 1586, El
Greco placed a medieval event in a
contemporary setting. The story is divided into
two separate parts. The bold lines, the
movement of the clouds and the strong folding
curves of the mantles of the angelic figures, give
the upper heavenly scene an emotional and
dramatic impact. Below, in the contemporary
world of mortals, the arrangement of the
figures is solemn and pious, with skillfully
rendered likenesses in the faces.*

El Greco

The last major Mannerist painter was the
Greek artist Domenikos Theotocopoulos
(1541–1614), who was born in Greece in
Crete. He was familiar with Byzantine art
from the years he lived in Crete. In Italy,
he came into contact with the art of
Michelangelo, Raphael and the Italian
Mannerists. He was trained in the Venetian school and at the age of twenty-five
worked there under Titian. His very personal style was formed before he went to
Toledo, Spain, where he was given the
nickname El Greco, which means "The
Greek." There, he developed his mature
work. His dramatic style and strong re-
jection of convention made his work
controversial and a target for hostile
criticism. While the figures and natural
forms in El Greco's paintings are still rec-
ognizable, he simplified and stylized
them so that they are nearly abstract.
This freedom to combine naturalistic representations and abstract forms is what
makes El Greco's work Mannerist. ■

By the end of second decade of the sixteenth century, the shock waves
of the religious Reformation in northern Europe, French invasion, the
end of Spanish domination and the sack of Rome in 1527, all led to
the loss of Italy's economic supremacy. Its optimistic and open artistic
climate came to an end. For the next two generations, the atmosphere
in Rome was bleak, austere and anti-artistic. Much of Italy had
become a battlefield, and later, so did most of Europe.

Reform within the Roman Catholic Church, the Counter-Reformation, was begun by Pope Julius II in 1512 at the Lateran Council,
called in response to the Reformation in northern Europe. Much later,
between 1545 and 1563, the Council of Trent defined the role of the
arts in the reformed Catholic community. The purpose of art was to
instruct people about their religious duties and about what they must
believe. Strict rules were to be applied to the representation of reli-

▲ *The influence of Michelangelo's* Last Judgment, *is evident in Giulio Romano's fresco for the Palazzo del Te*, The Fall of the Portico, *of 1532 to 1534.*

Pontormo's The Deposition *of 1526 to 1528, painted in oil on wood, recalls Michelangelo's obsession with the human figure. The figure of Christ seems, in his death, to beckon the viewer to enter the scene.* ▼

Giulio Romano and Mantua

Giulio Romano shook off the influence of Raphael and went to Mantua, in the service of the Duke of Mantua, in 1524, to take Andrea Mantegna's place for the decoration of the ducal palace. He produced frescoes in the Mannerist style for the Palazzo del Te at Mantua, between 1532 and 1534. The decoration of the rooms is conceived with brilliant solutions in perspective. The *Room of the Giants* was painted in one continuous sweep from the base of the walls, to the center of the ceiling vault. Giulio Romano also worked as an architect in the Mantua Cathedral to create a fine example of Mannerist interior church architecture. ■

gious stories. The clergy were to instruct and guide artists.

In spite of the Church's provisions, most artists active in Italy between about 1550 and 1590 rejected the earlier traditions of the Renaissance based on the classical values of antiquity and formal mathematical measurements. In Italy, the new style was called Mannerism. It appealed only to a small number of artists so Mannerism had a restricted influence and a limited audience.

In direct opposition to High Renaissance ideals, the Mannerists created a visionary world in their work, instead of a naturalistic one full of earthly realities. They emphasized the eccentric over the commonplace. Unrelated ideas, artificial concepts and distortion were often important elements in their work. From its beginnings in Italy, Mannerism spread to France, the Netherlands, Germany, England and Spain.

Those who opposed Mannerism in the late sixteenth century, declared that it was not the right sort of art for the Counter-Reformation. It had no realism, clarity and emotional vitality. It was too individualistic and fantastic to fit the needs of the Church.

The first major Mannerist artist in Rome, who painted frescoes on a grand scale, was Giulio Romano (approx. 1499–1546), Raphael's chief assistant. He completed many of Raphael's commissions for the Vatican. Jacopo Pontormo (1494–1571) was one of the first and most acclaimed Mannerists in Florence.

Mannerist sculpture is best represented by Benvenuto Cellini (1500–71). He was a Florentine sculptor, goldsmith and engraver and greatly admired Michelangelo, Raphael and classical sculptures. His early works make this clear. Cellini absorbed the Mannerist spirit of caprice and unrealistic elegance, while he was at Fontainebleau, in France, at the court of King Francis I (1494–1547), who ruled France between 1537 and 1547. His most admired works are his saltcellar for Francis I, made between 1539 and 1543, and the bronze *Perseus*, made between 1545 and 1554, in the Loggia dei Lanzi, Florence.

13 Baroque Art in Italy

▲ Judith Slaying Holofernes, *painted in oil on canvas about 1620, is a fine example of the dramatic power of Artemisia Gentileschi's pictures.*

The Renaissance exploration of the world continued throughout the sixteenth century. By the seventeenth century, a truly scientific spirit began to be expressed in Europe. Attention turned away from magic and the authority of the Church. People began to look for answers about the unknown and the unexplored through personal observation. The French philosopher, scientist and Roman Catholic René Descartes (1596–1650) replaced medieval faith with reason. The Italian Galileo Galilei (1564–1642) redefined the relationships between the sun, the earth and the planets. He and the Englishman Francis Bacon (1561–1626) began the experimental method of scientific investigation. The telescope was invented and perfected, thermometers were made, the circulation of the blood was discovered and many of the basic discoveries of physics were made.

The Roman Catholic Counter-Reformation took place at the same time. The Council of

▲ *Annibale Carracci was assisted in the huge project to decorate the Farnese Palace by his brother Agostino and his students from 1597 to 1604. The fresco's subject is the loves of the classical gods. It is a fine example of early Baroque monumental painting. This is a detail.*

Borromini's church architecture introduced a new approach to the use of spatial form and chiaroscuro. Borromini was fascinated by geometry which he used to design the church of St. Ivo. The exotic structure is beautifully related to the Renaissance courtyard. ▼

Ceiling Painting

The great ceiling paintings of the Italian Baroque period are its finest achievements. They give the appearance of infinite space. Brilliant color schemes and architectural perspective solutions like these had never been achieved before. Annibale Carracci (1560–1609) came to Rome from Bologna to decorate the gallery of the Farnese Palace. Carracci strove for a revival of classicism. His ceiling is exuberant and sensual with luminous, rich color. ■

Trent, which sat from 1545 to 1563, condemned abuses by priests, set up a system of supervision of priests and defined the correct doctrine of the Church. By 1563, a stable Roman Catholic church had been restored in Europe.

The Mannerist style was hardly suitable for the needs of the Church, as laid down by the Council of Trent. The spirit and work of the Church was to inspire religious awe in the hearts of an essentially illiterate people. Mannerism lacked the emotional intensity, realism and clarity which the Church needed.

From 1580 onward, art of the Counter-Reformation, Baroque art, began to appear. It had a broader and freer approach in showing religious subjects. Its aim was to move viewers. Baroque artists reconnected the world of the senses with the inner world of the spirit. They put art and nature together again. The dominating feature of Baroque works of art is dramatic movement. Sculpture was realistically modeled and poses were based on the S-curve to create twisting figures in

The Glorification of the ▶
Reign of Urban VIII, painted by Pietro da Cortona between 1633 and 1639, is a feast in visual imagery. It seduces the eye and stimulates the emotions. The fresco is divided into five separate scenes by a painted framework, on which painted stucco nudes are placed. The aim of the painted frame was to define the pictorial space. A double illusion was created by placing three-dimensional figures in this illusion of real space. Warm and cool colors create harmony.

Alessandro Algardi ___

Alessandro Algardi (1595–1654), followed in the footsteps of the great Bernini. He was another important Baroque sculptor. His representation in stone of *The Meeting of Pope Leo I and Attila* commemorated the traditionally miraculous defeat of the barbarian Huns led by Attila in 452. Much of Algardi's interpretation in the subject must have been influenced by Raphael's painting of the same subject at the Vatican. ■

Algardi's major work is the monumental illusionistic relief, made between 1646 and 1653, The Meeting of Pope Leo I and Attila. *He produced the illusion of depth in this complicated composition by graduating the projection of figures: the flatter they are the more they recede into the distance. Algardi's relief set a precedent, after which reliefs were often preferred to painting.* ▼

The Triumph of the ▶ Name of Jesus, *the ceiling decoration of the church of Gesù, is Giovanni Battista Gauli's (1639–1709), masterpiece. It thrusts the viewer into a deep, imaginary hole in the roof to the sky. Some of the figures, modeled in painted stucco, spill beyond the painting's margin casting real shadows.*

space. Painting offered the illusion of vast and deep space. Sometimes Baroque painters permitted their subjects to overflow the picture frame and to be transformed into sculptural images.

In 1585, Pope Sixtus V (1521–90) started a campaign to refurbish the city of Rome. Patronage was offered by the Church on a large scale. By the seventeenth century, there was intense building activity in Rome that attracted many talented architects. Most of the major works in Rome at the beginning of the seventeenth century came under the direction of the Lombard architect Carlo Maderno (1556–1629). Maderno enlarged St. Peter's Basilica by adding a nave to Michelangelo's original central plan. Maderno's projects were continued by Gian Lorenzo Bernini (1598–1680) who was responsible for most full-blown Roman Baroque architecture. Francesco Borromini (1599–1667) often worked with Bernini. He was among the great figures of the Roman Baroque.

St. Peter's ___

The great oval piazza of the Basilica of St. Peter was designed by Gian Lorenzo Bernini. This space embodies the very essence of the Baroque ideal. The viewer is overwhelmed by its immense scale. Without the presence of human figures, it is difficult to grasp the size of the entire complex of church and square. The return of symbolism is evident: the colonnades which enclose the piazza represent the all-embracing arms of the Church. The entire picture represents one hundred years of architecture by Italy's most significant architects: Michelangelo's 1547 dome, Maderno's façade of 1606 and Bernini's 1657 colonnade. ■

▲ *Bernini's* David *of 1623, is contained in a kind of pictorial space in which the viewer gets involved.*

Pietro Berrettini da Cortona (1596–1669) is the third famous Baroque architect and painter. Da Cortona used free-standing columns, like those in Brunelleschi's Florentine churches, not only as supports but also as important decoration.

Gian Lorenzo Bernini was the most prolific and greatest sculptor-architect of the Baroque period. Sculpture, painting and architecture have never been so closely related as they were during the Baroque period and Bernini was able to unite them in such a way that the viewer is free to move from one dimension to the other. His early works such as *David*, of 1623, have a Classicism and yet begin to invade the space around them.

In the first decade of the seventeenth century, painting in Rome was dominated by Caravaggio (approx. 1571–1610). He painted his subjects realistically and broke the accepted rules for religious art. His intention was to try to help the common man to identify with the subjects of his paintings despite the fact that most people wanted religious paintings to be idealized and not reflect their own lives. Nevertheless, Caravaggio's moving and realistic interpretations of religious events did receive the approval of important patrons. They also appealed to Protestants, and so Caravaggio's influence spread to northern Europe.

In Bernini's The Ecstasy of St. Theresa *(1645–52), the white marble of the figures loses its hard surface in the luminous atmosphere.* ▼

The Calling of St. Matthew, *painted in oil on canvas between 1599 and 1602, illustrates Caravaggio's contribution to religious subjects. His characters are painted realistically in contemporary dress.* ▼

14 Baroque Art in Flanders, Holland and Spain

Peter Paul Rubens

Peter Paul Rubens (1577–1640) was apprenticed to Flemish masters, and by the time he was twenty-one he developed his own style of painting. No other northern painter absorbed so completely the great High Renaissance works of Caravaggio and Carracci. Rubens could compete with the great Italian masters and, in some respects, surpassed them in developing deep space and light in painting. He is considered the most complete European painter, because he combined the best from Italian painting and northern European art. ■

▲ *In this early Rubens altarpiece,* The Raising of the Cross, *about 1609, a feeling of energy and emotion spreads through the picture.*

Art in Flanders in the seventeenth century was dominated by painting. The new Baroque style appeared in Flanders about fifty years later than Italy. Many Flemish carvers in stone and wood migrated to Italy, England, France, Holland and Germany to take up apprenticeships or to seek commissions wherever the new style was required.

In the sixteenth and seventeenth centuries, the monarchies in France, England and Spain were still dependent on the friendship, goodwill and support of the nobles, but during the end of the sixteenth century, these monarchies tried, with varying degrees of success, to centralize their power. They met resistance from the nobility and the middle classes. Revolts and civil war lasted until the second half of the seventeenth century. England, the most stable of the three countries, emerged politically as the most advanced state in Europe. Spain had accepted the loss of the northern part of the Low Countries with the formation of the United Provinces of the Netherlands, although Flanders remained subject to Spanish rule. The United Provinces had a relatively democratic constitution and Protestant Calvinism became the state religion.

Calvinism was restricting for the arts. No rich decoration was permitted and no decoration of any kind was allowed in churches. Except for the City Hall in Amsterdam there was no building on a grand scale in the Netherlands in the seventeenth century. Consequently, there was little need for sculpture or monumental works of art. Painting, however, flourished in every sector of society, particularly among the middle class which had begun collecting and commissioning art. The Netherlands was a nation of commerce. Merchants

Anthony van Dyck

Anthony van Dyck (1599–1641) became Rubens's assistant before he was twenty. He was so adept at imitating his master's technique that critics often argue over whether a painting is by Rubens or van Dyck. Van Dyck's style emerged more refined and elegant than Rubens's. He worked at the court of King Charles I (1600–49) of England from about 1620 to 1641. The painter's vibrant and quick use of the brush was responsible for an innovative tradition in portraiture in England that lasted for almost a hundred years. ■

◄ *Van Dyck's* Portrait of Jean Grusset Richardot and his Son, *in oil on canvas before 1623, was painted with a deftness of brushstroke.*

Frans Hals

Frans Hals (1580/85–1666) came from Antwerp and settled in Haarlem in the Netherlands. His capacity for using his brush with great speed and accuracy led to paintings full of freshness and vitality. In later life, Hals painted with a more severe hand. He continued the tradition of portrait painting of the sixteenth century. ■

Diego de Silva y Velázquez's (1599–1660) mature work, Maids of Honor, *painted in 1656 in oil on canvas, shows his capacity to penetrate human character.* ▼

and farmers collected art as paintings were considered good investments.

The liberalization of immigration laws meant that the Netherlands allowed in refugees escaping persecution and political exiles from all over Europe. It benefited from the new energy coming from other countries which stimulated intellectual and scientific advancement. The great increase in commissions for art was an important incentive for a variety of schools that sprang up throughout the country, such as those in Utrecht, Amsterdam, Leyden and Delft. Public demand for art had begun the previous century and there came to be a real art industry in the 1600s. The Baroque style was introduced to the Netherlands by way of the Catholic city of Utrecht where people were very attracted to Caravaggio's work.

Rembrandt van Rijn (1606–69) is the greatest of the Dutch painters. His genius was in his mastery of all the techniques of painting which he used to express his feeling about the human spirit. Rembrandt felt Caravaggio's influence. Like the Italian artist, he took a down-to-earth approach when creating religious art, as in *The Supper at Emmaus*, painted in oil on canvas in 1648. Rembrandt's concern for the poor and the persecuted is shown in the etching *Christ Preaching*, of 1652. He created a moving scene of human warmth and intimacy in this work.

The seventeenth century in Spain is considered its golden century artistically, under the rule of the last three Habsburg monarchs, Philip III, Philip IV and Charles II. Painting was of great importance at the court of Philip IV where Velázquez was chief court painter. He helped to define the the cultural atmosphere of Madrid where the Baroque style continued until the end of the eighteenth century.

Architecture and sculpture were mainly restricted to the needs of the Church. The façade of Granada Cathedral, of 1667, by Alonso Cano (1601–1667), painter, sculptor and architect, is considered the earliest Spanish Baroque masterpiece. The viewer's attention is drawn to the high arches that rise to the top of the façade and suggest oriental themes.

Rembrandt painted ► The Night Watch *in 1642. It marked a change of direction in his work. He defied the traditional use of centralizing lighting on important people and resorted to a freer, less orthodox, theatrical lighting.*

15 Baroque Art in Germany and Austria

Between 1618 and 1648, the Thirty Years' War caused a grave artistic setback to the countries involved in the conflict. The German principalities of Austria, Bohemia, Spain, France, the Netherlands, Denmark and Sweden were all affected. Most great palaces, monasteries, churches and civic structures were destroyed, though there was still sporadic building. In Germany the population was reduced from 16 million to 8 million people. Restoration work and a revival of artistic activity began after 1680 and continued to the end of the eighteenth century. The Austrian and German victory over the Turks in 1683, encouraged resurgence and reconstruction in the devastated lands.

Church of St. Charles Borromaeus

The great church of St. Charles Borromaeus was built in Karlskirche, Vienna between 1716 and 1737. In it a variety of styles taken directly from antiquity, the Renaissance and the new Baroque style are brought together. J.B. Fischer von Erlach (1656–1723) was the first important late Baroque architect in central Europe. His extraordinary talent succeeded in harmonizing the rich and imposing qualities of the different styles in the design of this church. ■

The new Baroque style of Italian art came to Germany and Austria, part of the Hapsburg Empire, as early as 1623 to 1629, with the Jesuits. This religious order built several important churches and colleges in Germanic territories. The Wallenstein Palace, at Prague, today in the Czech Republic, of 1625 to

▲ *Tiepolo's ceiling fresco of 1751 for the Kaisersaal,* Apollo Conducting Beatrice and Burgundy to Frederick Barbarossa, *begins abruptly at the oval frame with no attempt to extend the scene into the surrounding space. The enormous swathes of blue sky and clusters of clouds, occasionally interrupted by a partially hidden figure, create a romantic feeling of immense space. The total effect thrills the eye but the decorative work does not involve the viewer emotionally. Experts agree that this work shows Tiepolo's creative talents at their height.*

The Episcopal Palace and the Kaisersaal

The Episcopal palace at Würzburg, Germany, by the architect Balthasar Neumann (1687–1753) contains late German Baroque elements. Pilasters, columns, cornices and architraves are disguised by luxurious decoration, outlined in gold on a white background, a popular trend in decoration. In the dramatic oval hall, the Kaisersaal, the eye is drawn upward into huge, brilliant, spidery forms reaching the great oval-shaped ceiling, where the climax is the fresco by the Italian painter Giovanni Battista Tiepolo (1696–1770). Tiepolo is considered the last great Italian decorative painter. His fresco technique was revolutionary in the luminosity and spatial depth he achieved. This was one of the most important advances in fresco painting in the eighteenth century. ■

German Ceiling Frescoes

Eighteenth-century German ceiling fresco painting experimented with the many possibilities of perspective and space. Italian Baroque ceiling and wall painters depended on a single vanishing point and created a deep illusion of space with the help of architectural elements in their paintings. German artists, however, used several vanishing points in the same picture. The viewer could stand at different places in the church or palace to enjoy the fresco. The northern artists also made more use of the movement found in Venetian frescoes. They introduced a kind of distorted space giving it a spiral or whirling movement. This can be seen in the work of Cosmas Damian Asam (1686–1739) and his brother Egid Quirin Asam (1692–1750). ■

▲ *The dramatic use of atmospheric dark and light in* The Flight into Egypt, *shows the influence of Italian painters, particularly Tintoretto. Adam Elsheimer painted the scene in oil on copper in 1609.*

1629, is one of the earliest central European Baroque buildings. It is an example of building in central Europe at this period, when Italian architects were used. The Baroque style arrived much later in the century in the rest of central Europe and Germany. A purely German Baroque style began to emerge in about 1690 under Hapsburg dominance.

A German school of painting flourished in Frankfurt. The two important artists there were the still life painter, George Flegel (1563–1638) and Adam Elsheimer (1578–1610). Elsheimer's painting shows Dutch and French influences, particularly in his atmospheric, nocturnal pictures.

Woodcarving was a long established craft in German-speaking countries. It developed and prospered in the Baroque period and carved, wooden, religious figures were used in churches. The outstanding wood carver was the Bavarian Ignaz Günther, (1725–75) who produced beautiful, elegant figures.

Bronze and stone decorations were made for secular buildings. One of the best equestrian statues was made in Austria by George Raphael Donner (1693–1741). He also produced attractive bronzes for fountains and gardens.

◄ *Northern European artists introduced new ideas to the use of stucco. The Assumption of the Virgin was made between 1717 and 1725 by the Bavarian architect, sculptor and decorative painter Egid Quirin Asam who was influenced by Bernini's grand manner.*

16 Baroque Classicism in France

Nicolas Poussin

Nicolas Poussin (approx. 1593–1665) was the unrivaled French painter of the seventeenth century. Although he spent most of his career in Rome, he remained essentially French. Poussin's early works show how attracted he was to Venetian colors and sensuality. His late works are closer to the ideals of classical antiquity in their clarity of form and gesture. ■

Poussin's landscapes were idealized like the ▶ *heroic figures in his art. This solemn and calm scene,* Landscape with the Burial of Phocion, *was painted in oil on canvas in 1648.*

▲ *In Georges de La Tour's (1593–1652)* Joseph the Carpenter, *painted in oil on canvas in 1645, the artist shows only the essence of the forms in the light and leaves the viewer's imagination to invent the rest.*

Louis XIV (1638–1715), known as the Sun King, succeeded to the throne of France in 1643 at the age of five. After 1653, the French monarchy was made secure and assumed absolute centralized power. Louis grew to be a powerful leader. France also became powerful and Louis XIV was respected and feared in many European countries. He was suspected of planning to oust the Hapsburg emperors and make France the supreme power in Europe. Toward the end of the century, even though France sought to avoid war, the rest of Europe remained cautious and suspicious of him.

The seventeenth century shift of power from Spain to France revived the stagnant artistic spirit of the French school. It had been stifled during the religious wars of the previous century, particularly during the Protestant Huguenot uprising which ended in 1629. Under Louis XIV,

Landscapes of Claude Lorraine

Like Poussin, Claude Lorraine's (1600–82) career was spent in Rome. Unlike Poussin, his aim was to express the feeling of poetry which he found in the Roman countryside. Delicate light softens the edges of the planes receding into the far distance of his landscapes. They capture the way the soft, Mediterranean light transforms nature. The idealized scenes drew English painters into the world of landscape painting throughout the eighteenth century. Lorraine's vision is classical but does not have the precision of Poussin, because the viewer is permitted to drift and wander between luminous meadows and swelling shadows. ■

Seventeenth century French sculptors resisted the Italian Baroque. Pierre Puget (1622–94) is an exception. Puget carved Milo of Cortona *in marble between 1671 and 1683.*

The French Academy

Art academies all over Europe followed the curriculum of the seventeenth century French Academy. Students were required to copy the works of other masters. Older students drew from life and plaster cast models, taken from ancient Greek and Roman statues. ■

Poussinistes and *Rubénistes*

Toward the end of the seventeenth century, two opposing factions grew out of the French Academy. The rigid, restrictive rules to train young artists, developed by Lebrun, fell into decline. One faction, the *Poussinistes*, defended the theory that drawing appealed to the mind and was superior to color. The other faction, the *Rubénistes*, said color appealed to everyone and drawing could be appreciated only by experts and the educated few. ■

major and minor arts flourished again. A French style appeared, concentrated around the court. Architecture had been given a head start earlier in the century under Henry IV (1553–1610), but painting and sculpture had had to wait rather longer because all the major artists, such as Nicolas Poussin, Claude Lorraine and Moise Valentin, had gone to Italy, attracted by the Italian Baroque grand manner.

The influence of the Italian Renaissance lasted longer in France than in the rest of northern Europe. In France, the Renaissance tradition of humanist thought and teaching was firmly embedded, and intellectual reasoning had become an absolute virtue. The Baroque style came into use in France in the seventeenth century, but there were artists who held firm to classicist ideals of form and composition. They wanted balance, harmony and clarity. They believed that color should be added to form and not given the same or a greater value than drawing. They believed art should be of the mind rather than the senses. The sculptures of Algardi, discussed in chapter thirteen, and the decorative work at Versailles, by Charles Lebrun (1619–90), were a compromise of the two styles. This compromise is referred to as Baroque Classicism.

The building and decoration of the immense Palace of Versailles, begun in 1661, was Louis XIV's greatest architectural undertaking. Work continued uninterrupted for thirty years. The architecture at Versailles shows Baroque characteristics, despite French reluctance to accept the style. Inside the palace, Louis XIV wanted a richly adorned background for himself and his court.

Charles Lebrun, the director of the French Royal Academy of Painting and Sculpture, oversaw the decoration of the palace, and, indeed, controlled artistic standards throughout the country. He combined all the arts in his brilliant conceptions for the extraordinary and resplendent interiors at Versailles.

◄ *The* Salon de la Guerre *at Versailles was decorated in 1678. Lebrun used sculpture, painting and interior design to achieve the stunning effect.*

17 Rococo Art

Pilgrimage to Cythera *is one of Watteau's* ▶
last works. He painted it in oil on canvas in
1717. In it Watteau attempted to join theater
and life. The settings of his pictures are often
taken from the Italian theater, the French
theater and the gardens of Versailles.
Classical myths also played a part in his
paintings. This one shows the young
lovers who have come to the mythological
island of love, Cythera.

The Salon de la Princesse at the Hotel de
Soubise in Paris, by the architect Gabriel-
Germain Boffrand (1667–1754), begun in
1732, is a fine example of the Rococo style.
The atmosphere is airy and light. The elaborate
decoration of the ceiling and frescoes add to the
refinement of the room. ▼

After Louis XIV's death in 1715, a change took place in French society and art. The court could move about more freely and independently. It moved from Versailles to Paris where the nobility lived in grand houses. There was less space for frescoes and opulent decoration, but more freedom of invention and personal fantasy went into the decoration of the interiors.

In England, the reign of George I (1660–1727), saw the beginnings of a constitutional monarchy. This development helped set the example of refinement and manners in England. The nobility and upper classes, more than the king's court, encouraged the development of the arts as an expression of social life as in France.

A new style, Rococo, grew out of the Baroque and began in France. It later spread to England. It did not strive for the discipline of classicism but aimed to please with its light touch.

Jean Antoine Watteau

Jean Antoine Watteau (1684–1721) was the most important figure in eighteenth century French painting. His art drew on several European styles including Baroque color, Flemish naturalism and Italian Renaissance. His success lay in his ability to put these styles together with Rococo spirit. He was able to develop the characters of his figures with great insight. His paintings emphasize the conflicting rules of the classical school of Poussin and the robust, vigorous qualities of the followers of Rubens. His last works put theater and life together, for example *Joli Gilles*, painted in 1719. ■

Much seventeenth-century English painting was produced by artists from abroad such as the Flemish painter Anthony van Dyck and German born Peter Lely (1618–80). After settling in London in 1643, Lely became the official court painter. He was influenced by van Dyck's art, but changed his style to please his royal clients.

William Hogarth (1697–1764) combined satire on the pomposity of the Rococo style with a concern for moral subjects. He used a robust and lively technique. Hogarth trained as a silversmith's apprentice and continued his career as an engraver and book illustrator. After 1720, he began to publish his popular prints.

After 1750, portrait painting in England was dominated by

▲ *Thomas Gainsborough painted* The Morning Walk *of 1786 in oil on canvas with generous brushwork that gives the subjects of this work vitality.*

▲ *Hogarth's pictures were morality plays intended to teach middle class values and expose the corruption and dissipation of English life. The painter criticized society and, at the same time, entertained the viewer with lively and colorful images. Social criticism appeared in Hogarth's paintings for the first time. This is* The Orgy *from* The Rake's Progress *of about 1734.*

Thomas Gainsborough and Joshua Reynolds. Thomas Gainsborough (1727–88) painted what he saw and what he admired. His style was light and flashy. He did not attempt to show the sitter's inner feelings, but their position in society.

Joshua Reynolds (1723–92) was Gainsborough's rival. He painted portraits idealizing his sitter rather than painting what he saw. He was president of the Royal Academy from its inception in 1768.

◀ *This is Joshua Reynolds's portrait of* Mrs. Siddons as the Tragic Muse. *The sitter's pose is like that of a Greek goddess.*

18 Neo-Classic Art

The Changing Scene

At the end of the eighteenth century, momentous events occurred in Europe and America. Russia's power extended to the Black Sea by 1793. Poland was partitioned between Russian, Prussia and Austria in 1795. The American Revolution began in 1776, followed by the French Revolution in 1789. The Industrial Revolution was underway and Robert Fulton's steamship made its first voyage in 1807. The modern era had arrived, but it was almost another century before the modern movement in art began. ■

▲ *The interest aroused by painting in the late eighteenth century was due mainly to its storytelling and moral content, rather than its style. Jean-Baptiste Greuze (1725–1805) was a genre painter in the manner of Hogarth. In* The Village Bride, *which he painted in oil on canvas in 1761, he supported Jean Jacques Rousseau's teachings on social justice and morality, by showing the simplicity, naturalness, honesty and virtue of the poor.*

The Neo-Classical and Romantic styles in art appeared alongside each other between 1750 and 1850. Neo-Classicism is sometimes seen as an early phase of Romanticism. Many artists moved from one style to the other, beginning their careers as Neo-Classicists and ending as Romantics.

The great European cultural manifestation called the Enlightenment

▲ *Jean Antoine Houdon (1741–1828), the most important French sculptor of the Neo-Classical period produced* Voltaire *in 1781. His work looked back to Roman portraiture.*

The Encyclopedia

In the middle of the eighteenth century, Jean d'Alembert (1717–83) and Denis Diderot (1713–84) completed an encyclopedia embracing the whole of human knowledge at the time. Many scholars contributed their knowledge and time. The first volumes of the encyclopedia were published in 1751. In spite of royal censorship, it was very popular. By the early 1770s, the work of nearly thirty volumes was completed. It offered the reader the thoughts and critical writings of the Enlightenment. ■

▲ *This is Angelica Kauffman's elegant portrait of Franciska Krasinska, the Duchess of Courland, painted about 1785. The sitter is portrayed like an ancient goddess.*

Jean Paul Marat (1743–93) was one of the leaders of the French Revolution. He was murdered in his bath tub. The sensational scene, The Death of Marat, *was executed in oil on canvas by Jacques-Louis David in a style influenced by Caravaggio's realism in 1793.* ▼

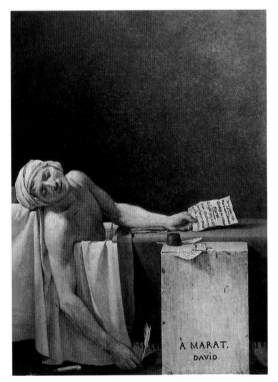

Angelica Kauffman _____

Angelica Kauffman (1741–1807) was a rare woman artist of her time and one of the most important Neo-Classical painters in England. Born in Switzerland, she became a founding member of the Royal Academy in London. She produced narrative paintings in a delicate style reminiscent of the Rococo and some fine, elegant portraits. Her paintings were often engraved and reproduced to decorate art objects. ■

encompassed the period from the end of seventeenth century through the entire eighteenth century. The French writer and philosopher Voltaire (1694–1778), the Swiss born Rousseau (1712–78) and the Scottish philosopher David Hume (1711–76) were part of the Enlightenment in Great Britain and France. They believed that all questions about human affairs and rights should be settled by reasoned argument about how to bring improvement to people's lives, instead of by appealing to tradition and the accepted authorities. Neo-Classical artists were drawn to these great thinkers and this was reflected in their art. Their art went against what was considered by some critics to be the decadent French Rococo style.

The spiritual center of Neo-Classicism was in Rome, where there was a strong reaction, lasting to the end of the 1700s, to the sweetened and soft expressions of the late Baroque. The sensational excavations at Pompeii and Herculaneum in the middle of the eighteenth century, attracted artists from northern Europe to Italy. There they became involved in Baroque Classicism and the renewed interest in antiquity. The excavations revealed details about everyday Roman life and the arts and crafts of the ancient Romans. Books with illustrations of new archeological finds were published and attracted general attention. France and England were the first countries to send archeologists and historians to the sites. Interest spread through Europe and by mid-century there was a lively revival of research.

A return to nature, morality and reason was the cry of the eighteenth century. Artists interpreted this as a return to the ancients, since they believed that the ancient Greeks were the first philosophers to discuss the concept of reason. Jacques-Louis David (1748–1825) is the best example of such an artist. He was the painter closest to the revival of Poussin's classicism. Their styles were similar. David's stay in Rome from 1775 to 1781 gave him an introduction to both the works of Caravaggio and the Neo-Classical style. David was involved in the political and social changes of his age, taking an active part in the French Revolution. His most accomplished work is the revolutionary *The Death of Marat* of 1793.

19 The Romantic Movement in Art

English Landscape Painting

Landscape painting in England was like a breath of fresh air sweeping through the English Royal Academy. John Constable (1776–1837) painted great landscapes and skies, capturing nature's generous settings and atmosphere. His paintings are convincing and believable to the extent that the viewer can accept his exaggerated and emotional, Romantic interpretation. He was highly respected in England and particularly in France during his lifetime. ■

In The Admiral's House on Hampstead Heath, *John Constable set this view of Admiral Matthew Barton's house, painted in oil on canvas in 1819, against an enormous English sky. He has captured the precise moment when the clouds have allowed the sunlight to filter through and illuminate the building.* ▼

▲ The Third of May 1808, *painted in oil on canvas between 1814 and 1815, shows Francisco Goya's expressive brushwork and use of light. It is a superb example of early Romanticism.*

The Enlightenment inspired interest in natural phenomena, logic and rationalism. It also unleashed an emotionalism that inspired the Romantic movement. At its height between 1790 and 1830, the Romantic movement influenced both art and literature.

Romantic artists gave free rein to their emotions. They rebelled against authority, established social rules and organized religion. They honored nature's ever-changing, wild characteristics. Their cause was liberty and their goal was individualism. The Romantics were

Upheaval and Change

As the Industrial Revolution gathered momentum in Europe, a social and cultural upheaval was inevitable. In 1815, Napoleon (1769–1821) had been defeated and exiled. The Greeks declared independence from the Turks in 1822. The July Revolution took place in France in 1830. There were political and social reforms in Great Britain between 1832 and 1835. Famine caused mass emigration from Ireland in 1846. In 1848 the Second Republic began in France. There were uprisings in Italy, Austria, Hungary and Germany. ■

◀ *Delacroix's* The Massacre at Chios, *completed in oil on canvas in 1824, seems to flash with many figures appearing and disappearing in the dramatic Romantic light.*

▲ *Ingres painted* Odalisque, *in oil on canvas in 1814. It is a visual feast. The artist rendered voluptuous flesh and convincing textures.*

Antonio Canova

The origins of the Romantic Movement in Neo-Classicism are reaffirmed in the work of the renowned Italian sculptor, Antonio Canova (1757–1822). He was born in Venice and worked in Rome. Canova's art puts the mind above the emotions, but there is a sensuality that comes to the surface and stirs the viewer's emotions. The *Borghese Venus*, which he carved in marble in 1808, offers the observer a mixture of early Romanticism and a touch of Rococo. The sitter Pauline Borghese is represented as the figure of Venus. ■

▲ *Turner envisioned a tragedy, reported in the newspapers, of slaves being cast into the sea, because of disease or to lighten the ship during storms, when he painted* The Slave Ship *in oil on canvas in 1840.*

concerned with naturalness and directness but they accepted the rules and methods of Neo-Classicism. Some of the themes of their paintings found inspiration in literature.

The Spanish painter Francisco Goya (1746–1828) worked at the Spanish court of Charles IV (1748–1819). He demonstrated his technical skill, as a master of the early Romantic period, in the great family portrait, *The Family of Charles IV*, painted in oil on canvas in 1800. The artist skillfully assimilated the Baroque qualities of Rembrandt and Velázquez and combined them in a personal style. He used fresh and dazzling brushstrokes that rivaled the best Baroque painters. He painted his models with frankness and a penetrating, unforgiving eye.

Jean-Auguste-Dominique Ingres (1780–1867) a pupil of David, had early success as a portrait painter. He believed that drawing was the basis of all great art. He was the chief opponent of the spreading Romantic movement. Ingres's paintings reveal a detached observation of their subjects. Although he never painted to achieve a Romantic sense of emotion, his paintings, such as *Odalisque* of 1814, show his interest in the supple and sensual modeled forms that appealed to Romantic taste.

Eugène Delacroix (1798–1863), on the other hand, was an unashamed Romantic who opposed Ingres's ideas. Although he strongly supported the Classical tradition, his use of color and exotic, emotion-charged subjects show he was the greatest of the French Romantic painters.

The work of the English painter, Joseph Mallord William Turner (1775–1851), captured the essence of the Romantic movement. Nature is the central focus of his work. The subject matter is merely suggested and touches the viewer's emotions. The swelling and all-embracing space seems to extend beyond the picture frame. With Turner's last works the Romantic era came to a close.

Bibliography

Avery, Charles. *Florentine Renaissance Sculpture.* New York and London: John Murray, 1970.

Bazin, Germain. *Baroque and Rococo.* New York and London: Thames and Hudson, 1964.

Berger, Franzsepp Wurten. *Mannerism: The European Style of the 16th Century.* New York, Holt, Rinehart and Winston, 1963.

Hoyghe, Rene, general ed. *Art and Mankind—Larousse Encyclopedia of Byzantine and Medieval Art.* 1963 ed. New York and London: Paul Hamlyn, 1963.

Janson, H.W. *History of Art.* 4th Ed. New York: Harry N. Abrams; New York and London: Thames and Hudson, 1991.

Martin, John Rupert. *Baroque.* Icon Editions. New York: Harper and Row, 1977.

Talbot Rice, David *The Dark Ages.* New York and London: Thames and Hudson, 1963.

White, John. *Art and Architecture in Italy 1250-1400.* The Pelican History of Art. New York and London: Penguin Books, 1987.

Wittkower, Rudolf. *Art and Architecture in Italy, 1600-1750.* The Pelican History of Art. New York and London: Penguin Books, 1980.

Glossary

abstract art Art that does not represent things realistically.

allegory A story in which people, objects, events have symbolic meaning.

apse A semicircular or polygonal recessed space in a building, generally a church, which has a dome for a roof.

architrave The main beam that rests on a capital or column.

atrium The central court of a Roman house. Also the portico in front of the main doors of a church.

baptistery The place, especially in a church, used for baptizing people.

buttress A structural support usually made of brick or stone that adds strength to a wall.

capital The decorative element at the top of a column.

chancel The part of a church around the altar reserved for the clergy and choir.

chapel A small church.

colonnade A series of columns.

cornice A horizontal, ornamental molding running around the wall of a room or crowning a building.

crusade A Christian military expedition to liberate the Holy Land from the Muslims in the eleventh through thirteenth centuries.

cupola A small dome or similar structure placed on a roof.

dome A rounded roof or ceiling of a building.

ecclesiastic A clergyman.

engraving A technique in which an image is scratched into a metal plate or piece of wood. It can then be used to print many copies of the image.

etching A printing technique in which a metal plate is engraved with an image using acid. It can then be used to print many copies.

fresco A type of painting made on wet plaster.

frieze A horizontal band of decoration.

genre Pictures which represent everyday life.

hierarchy A group of people or things arranged in order of rank, class or grade.

icon A sacred image.

illusionism In art, a way of representing objects or space in a painting so realistically that the objects or space appear to be real and not painted representations.

jamb The side of a doorway or window frame.

lithography A printing process using a stone or a metal plate specially treated so parts of the surface repel ink.

mosaic A pattern or picture assembled from small pieces of colored stone or tile pressed into soft mortar.

motif The main idea in an artistic composition.

nave The main part of a church.

perspective A way of representing objects or figures in a work of art to show relative distance or depth.

reliquary A receptacle for relics.

sarcophagus A stone coffin usually decorated with sculpture.

tesserae Small pieces of stone or tile that are used to make mosaics.

vault An arched roof or ceiling.

Photo Credits

Academy, Florence: 36 left

Alte Pinakothek, Munich: 51 right

Antwerp Cathedral: 48

Archeology Society, Avesnes, France: 20

Archepiscopal Museum, Ravenna: 13 bottom left

courtesy Arena Chapel, Padua: 26 right

Baptistery, Florence: 29 top

Baptistery, Pisa: 25 left

Barberini Palace, Rome: 45 bottom right

Borghese Gallery, Rome: 47 top left

Brancacci Chapel, Santa Maria del Carmine, Florence: 30 right

Trustees of the British Museum: 18

Cathedral Saint-Lazare, Autun, France: 23 top

Chartres Cathedral: 24, 25 right

Church of Angoulême, Angoumois, France: 23 bottom

Church of the Gesù, Rome: 46 right

Church of Saint Bavo, Ghent, Belgium: 40 bottom left

Church of Saint Michael, Hildesheim: 17 right

Reproduced by permission of the City of Bayeux, France: 19 top

Cliché des Musées de Versailles, 41 right

Department of Archaeology, Durham University: 14 left

Fabre Museum, Montpellier, France: 56 left

Galleria dell'Accademia, Venice: 35 right

Hotel de Soubise, Paris: 54 left

The Kaisersaal, Wurzburg: 50

Kunsthistorisches Museum, Vienna: 33 left, 40 top left

Lascaux Museum: 8

Lateran Museum, Rome: 11 right

The Louvre, Paris: 34 left, 49 top left, 52 left and right, 53 top, 54 right, 56 right, 59 top left and right

Musée Condé, Chantilly, France: 27

Musée d'Aquitaine, Bordeaux: p. 9 bottom

Musée des Beaux Arts, Dijon: 28 bottom left

Musée d'Unterlinden, Colmar, France: 40 right

Musées Royaux des Beaux-Arts de Belgium, Brussels: 57 bottom

Museum of Fine Arts, Boston: 28 top left, 41 bottom left, 59 bottom left

The National Gallery, London: 33 right, 38, 55 top left

National Museum, Florence: 29 bottom

National Gallery, Rome: 41 top left

Or San Michele, Florence: 30 left

Palace of Versailles: 53 bottom

Palazzo del Té, Mantua: 43 top

Palazzo Farnese, Rome: 45 top left

The Pierpont Morgan Library, New York: 17 top

Pompeii Museum: 10

The Prado, Madrid: 28 right, 39, 49 bottom left, 58 right

Private Collection: 9 top, 11 top left, 12, 14 right, 15 top and bottom, 16, 17 bottom, 19 bottom, 21 left and right, 22, 31 left, 35 left, 45 bottom left, 51 left, 55 bottom left, 57 top, 58 left

Rijksmuseum, Amsterdam: 49 right

San Lorenzo, Florence: 37 top left

Santa Costanza, Rome: 11 bottom left

Santa Felicita, Florence: 43 bottom

Santa Maria delle Grazie, Milan: 34 right

Santa Maria della Vittoria, Cornaro Chapel, Rome: 47 bottom left

Courtesy Sant'Apollinare in Classe: 13 top left

Sant'Apollonia, Florence: 32 top

San Francesco, Arezzo: 31 right

San Luigi dei Francesi, Rome: 47 right

Santo Tome, Toledo, Spain: 42

San Vitale, Ravenna: 13 right

Sir John Soane's Museum, London: 55 right

Uffizi Gallery, Florence: 26, 32 bottom, 44

The Vatican, Rome: 36 right (Sistine Chapel), 37 bottom left (Vatican Palace), 46 left (Saint Peter's)

Villa Farnesina, Rome: 37 right

Index